The Church in Revolutionary Times

An Illustrated History of the Church

Created and Produced by Jaca Book

An outline by chapter can be found on the last two pages of this volume.

The Church in Revolutionary Times

An Illustrated History of the Church

From 1700 to 1850

Translated and adapted by John Drury
Illustrated by Franco Vignazia

 Winston Press   430 Oak Grove   Minneapolis, Minnesota 55403

Published in Italy under the title
L'epoca delle rivoluzioni: La chiesa e la sua storia
Copyright © 1979 Editoriale Jaca Book.

**Licensed publisher and distributor
of the English-language edition:**
  Winston Press, Inc.
  430 Oak Grove
  Minneapolis, Minnesota 55403
  United States of America

Agents:
Canada—
  LeDroit/Novalis-Select
  135 Nelson St.
  Ottawa, Ontario
  Canada K1N 7R4

Australia, New Zealand, New Guinea, Fiji Islands—
  Dove Communications, Pty. Ltd.
  Suite 1, 60–64 Railway Road
  Blackburn, Victoria 3130
  Australia

United Kingdom, Ireland, and South Africa—
  Fowler-Wright Books, Ltd.
  Burgess St.
  Leominster, Herefordshire
  England

Created and produced by Jaca Book, Milan
Color selection: Mediolanum Color Separations
Printing: Gorenjski tisk, Kranj

History Consultant: The Rev. Marvin R. O'Connell
                Professor of History, University of Notre Dame
Winston Staff: Florence Flugaur, Cyril A. Reilly—editorial
                Chris Larson, Keith McCormick—design

Library of Congress Catalog Card Number: 79-67838
ISBN: 0-86683-158-4

5 4 3 2 1

An Illustrated History of the Church

The Church in Revolutionary Times

Introduction

When the eighteenth century began, the Christians of Europe had to admit that the religious unity their ancestors had known was gone beyond any hope of recovery. They were now permanently splintered into competing denominations, and they had brought their divisions with them to the far corners of the earth which they had conquered and settled. Moreover, they discovered at about the same time that new ideas were developing which, though often good and even noble as far as they went, called into question the fundamental belief, shared by Catholics, Orthodox and Protestants, that human beings are called by God to supernatural life. Many thoughtful people came to adopt these "enlightened" ideas as a substitute for Christianity, and some of the more extreme among them, like the famous Voltaire, urged that Christianity be destroyed in order to promote human happiness.

This period is called the Enlightenment, or the Age of Reason. European monarchs liked to think of themselves as "enlightened" rulers who governed their countries with reasonable and efficient laws. Increasingly, however, their subjects came to see them as despots who trampled upon human rights. Resistance to them grew until it exploded in the American and French revolutions, which ushered in the new political age when popular democracy would become the most important form of government. The revolutionary movement spread all over Europe and Latin America, and with it went another kind of revolution, the Industrial Revolution, which in its own way did much to change people's habits, customs, values, and loyalties. By 1850, only Russia stood firm for the old "enlightened despotism."

The Christian Church was particularly challenged during these times of violent change. As political, economic, and social structures altered swiftly and dramatically, Christians had to adapt themselves to the noble ideals of the Enlightenment and the Revolution without surrendering to the excesses of those movements. They realized that respect for reason must not exile God from the universe he has made; that respect for freedom must not end in a reign of terror.

Marvin R. O'Connell

1. At the beginning of the eighteenth century, the Christian world seemed divided beyond repair.

By 1700 Europe had been divided on matters of the Christian religion for almost two hundred years, and the restoration of unity seemed unlikely.

Roman Catholicism had won out in Spain, Italy, southern Germany, Poland, Austria, Croatia, Bohemia, the Spanish Netherlands, and Ireland. It was also the majority Church in France, Hungary, and parts of Switzerland. In England, the majority Church was Anglican, a large minority was Protestant, and a tiny minority was Roman Catholic. Lutheranism was very strong in Germany and the Scandinavian countries. Scotland was almost entirely Calvinistic, and there were Calvinists in Hungary and parts of Germany. They were the majority in parts of Switzerland and were a large minority in France and England. And Calvinists ruled the United Provinces of the

Netherlands. Farther east, the Russian and Greek Orthodox Churches went their own way. They were not much involved with the issues affecting western Christians.

European missionaries and colonies carried the religious divisions of western Europe to other continents as well. Roman Catholics had visited Asia and had settled Latin America. Catholic Portuguese had mainly settled the central portion of Africa, while Dutch Calvinists had explored the southern part of that continent. Explorers and settlers in North America included French and Spanish Catholics, French Huguenots, English Anglicans and Puritans, and members of many smaller sects.

The religious climate was one of unquestioning confidence in the correctness of one's own beliefs often combined with outer suspicion and sometimes even hatred toward Christians who held different views. And other changes in the outlook of some people raised new questions, as we shall see in the next chapter.

2. Beginning around 1650, new views arose about the universe, religious life, the world, and the relation of people to the world. Among some people, this led to a revolution in thought. This movement, which became very obvious in the 1700s, is called the Enlightenment.

During the fifteenth and sixteenth centuries, the medieval Christian outlook in Europe had slowly changed. People borrowed from the past to fashion their own present. The writings of ancient Greek and Roman philosophers and statesmen were rediscovered. Studying these writings led some humanists to form a different view of life. In most cases, these humanists remained Christian, but their views did differ from those of earlier Christian thinkers.

Then, in the 1500s, the Protestant Reformation put an end to the church unity of western Europe. At the same time, many other things were happening: Explorers were discovering unknown continents; scientists were figuring out a new view of the whole universe; strong rulers were organizing their states; and

businessmen were establishing new ways to ship their goods and obtain payment for them. There were many new things to see and do, new ways to solve problems, new ideas to think about.

Most people still clung to and practiced their religious faith. But some people claimed that nature and natural law were more important than revealed religion and belonging to a church. Such people as Copernicus, Galeleo, Kepler, Descartes, and Newton had formed a new picture of the world. Knowledge was power, it now seemed, and many intellectuals had unbounded confidence in human reason. They held that human reason could show human beings how to live happily and successfully. In this view, then, there was no need for God, religious faith, or churches. Organized

religion, some thinkers believed, was mere superstition and should be destroyed.

These various strands of thought were knit together in the 1700s and resulted in a movement known as the Enlightenment. It is also known as the Age of Reason because of the increased emphasis on logical thinking. Two basic ideas in the Enlightenment were freedom of inquiry and freedom in decision-making. The Enlightenment took many different forms, some of which are described in this book. Many people in Europe were affected by the Enlightenment only slowly, if ever. But after the Enlightenment, the outlook of western Europeans was different than it had been before.

3. Increased travel influenced western Europe in the 1700s. Besides seeing new things and meeting new people, Europeans could now read reports about other parts of the world. One famous report was that of Father Lafiteau, a missionary to North America.

In the 1700s, increased travel brought Europeans into contact with unfamiliar peoples and customs in Asia and the Americas. At the same time, the printing press began to be more widely used, and the many stay-at-homes were able to read accounts of foreign voyages, distant lands, and cultures far different from that of Europe. Europeans had tended to believe that their religion and culture were superior. Now when they learned that beliefs differed from one area of the world to the next, some Europeans felt that it was not easy to decide which ones were right and true.

Missionaries traveled the world to spread the Christian faith. Some of them realized that the cultures of the people they visited should be treated with respect and love. The reports of such missionaries often stated or implied criticism of the way that Europeans behaved in distant lands. Some missionaries saw that the Christian faith should not be too closely tied to the culture of western Europe. For example, Jesuit reports about the Chinese culture showed that China was an old and highly civilized country that seemed to get along very well without Christianity. Such a report was welcomed by those Enlightenment thinkers who were hostile to the Church.

But reports about belief in God among seemingly primitive people could be inspiring to faithful Christians. Father Lafiteau, a Jesuit, brought back to Europe with him examples of the ceremonial masks used by the Indians he visited. He also wrote a famous set of reports about the Iroquois and Huron Indians of North America. He suggested that they seemed to have some basic notion about divine revelation. To many people, this understanding of God proved that primitive peoples were not atheists—that they did believe in God.

4. In the late 1600s and early 1700s, the doctrine of Jansenism was debated in France. Jansenism taught that even before a person is born, God has decided whether that person is to be damned or saved.

In 1713, the pope rejected Jansenism. This caused serious division in the French Catholic Church.

In the 1600s, the views of Bishop Jansen created much argument in the French Catholic Church. After examining the writings of St. Augustine on God's grace, Jansen had reached the conclusion that each human being is destined in advance by God for salvation or damnation. This doctrine is known as predestination, and the bishop's teachings were called Jansenism. Arguments about Jansenism raged in France. Many people were devoted students and followers of St. Augustine's views, and Bishop Jansen had claimed to be presenting these views. Debate over Jansenism became a political issue, too, because there were arguments between the pope in Rome and the French king. People and clergy took sides, and debate went on.

In 1713 Pope Clement XI signed the bull or decree that rejected Jansenism. The papal decree was not well received in France. Many churchmen, theologians, and lay people felt that it also attacked the views of St. Augustine, one of the great Christian thinkers. Soon the French bishops and members of religious orders were divided into those who accepted the papal decree and those who did not. Many Jansenistic parish priests would not read their bishop's instructions in church if the bishop favored the papal decree. A serious conflict raged in the French Church, with many good people on each side.

King Louis XIV had agreed to force the acceptance of the papal decree, but it was a harder job than he had expected. When the king died (1715), Philip of Orleans became regent, ruling in place of the boy-king, Louis XV. Philip favored Jansenism and he permitted many priests and bishops to withdraw the approval that Louis XIV had forced them to give to the papal decree. Angry debate in words and printed publications continued.

Some bishops and lay people began to call for a church council, hoping to revoke the condemnation of Jansenism. The regent, now worried about the seriousness of the quarrel, tried to discourage those calling for a council, and he tried to impose silence on both parties. But he did not succeed. Indeed, it came to the point where some government workers, in order to hold their jobs, had to get a paper from their pastor to prove that they had made their Easter confession to a non-Jansenistic priest.

When King Louis XV grew old enough to rule in his own name, he took a stronger line of action and managed to silence both sides.

5. In France in the early 1700s,
The Convulsionaries excited
much interest and attention.
Religious feelings aroused
strong emotions in these
people, sometimes leading
to convulsions, prophecies,
and cures that could not
be explained. During these
same years, another—and
deeply spiritual—kind of
religious piety was being
lived in Europe. Among
them was the Society
of Friends (Quakers).

At this time, people were feeling more confidence in human reason and the five senses as
sources or tools of knowledge. This feeling was
shared by scientists, writers, and many others.
But it was not the only feeling evident among
people of the day.

There was also a keen interest in wonders
that could not be explained by human reason.
One proof of this was the interest of many people in the events surrounding the Convulsionaries of Saint-Médard. Saint-Médard was
the name of a church in Paris to which a small
cemetery was attached. Francis of Paris
(1690-1727), a man who had won great respect
for his saintly life and his charity towards the
poor, was buried there. In 1731 some sick people visiting his grave were somehow cured and
went into convulsions. Similar incidents happened again and again. The police closed the
cemetery, but the convulsions did not stop.
Some people went to private homes, gathered
around a crucifix or some other religious object, and worked themselves into a sort of
trance and made prophecies.

Many of the people involved were Jansenists, though not all Jansenists were necessarily on the side of the Convulsionaries. Many devout Jansenists criticized what was going on among the Convulsionaries. But the odd and unexplainable events were sometimes presented as divine signs that the papal decree condemning Jansenism should be rejected.

In spite of these unusual practices, normal religious devotions and activities continued. Devout people in cloisters and monasteries continued to seek mystical union with God, and lay people of all religions tried to develop their spiritual life and practice it every day.

However, new religious developments were seen in various countries of Europe. Among them were Pietism, Methodism (both described in later chapters), and the Society of Friends (Quakers).

The Society of Friends (Quakers) originally "the Friends of Truth," was organized by George Fox in 1652 in England. Quakers respect and use the Bible but they believe that God's word continues to be revealed to those who listen. They call this personal revelation the "Inner Light" which is the Holy Spirit working in each person. George Fox's ideal was "to walk cheerfully over the earth speaking to that of God in everyone."

Quaker Meetings for Worship are held in unadorned rooms in silence, which is broken when a Friend feels "led" to pray or to share an inspired message. Since Friends believed that Christ sat with them in Meeting, they had no ordained clergy. Outside of Meeting, they did not remove their hats, even when in the presence of worldly authority such as kings or judges. They refused to take oaths saying that their custom was to speak the truth while taking an oath presumed that they had been lying.

If their Inner Light so directed, Quakers did not take part in war or military service. Thus they were often in trouble with authorities and sometimes put into prison. When William Penn established a colony called Pennsylvania in 1682, there was religious freedom for all.

6. Among Roman Catholics, devotion to Jesus under the title "The Sacred Heart of Jesus" spread rapidly during this time. This devotion was started by John Eudes and helped by Margaret Mary Alacoque. Though opposed by some theologians, the devotion was widely accepted by the people.

Emphasis on the power of reason in the eighteenth century did not prevent new developments in religious feeling. But there was more suspicion of mystical experiences than in earlier times. Earlier mystics often had attracted attention quickly, and their lives would be told in sermons and books. Now even Roman Catholics paid less attention to what was going on in secluded convents and monasteries. But the mystical life continued among such orders as the Visitation nuns, and Jesuit spiritual writers remained popular.

One of the newer developments in Roman Catholic piety around this time was devotion to the Sacred Heart. This old religious practice was popularized in the 1600s by John Eudes, an Oratorian priest from Normandy. John built seminaries, preached tirelessly, and founded the Company of Jesus and Mary. He came to see the human heart of Jesus as the symbol of God's love for human beings. To him, Jesus' heart summed up and represented the chief mysteries of Christianity: creation, incarnation, redemption, and God's summons to all Christians to show repentance for their sins. In the houses of his Company, Eudes established the feast of the Sacred Heart. In 1670 he composed a liturgy or prayers for a Mass in honor of the Sacred Heart of Jesus.

Very probably this new devotion would not

have made much of an impression on Roman Catholics if it had not been for a French Visitation nun named Margaret Mary Alacoque. She reported that Jesus had appeared to her and told her to help spread "the flame of his love." Jesus, she said, wanted the faithful to see and venerate an image of his heart surrounded by thorns and topped by a cross. One phrase from her vision became well known: "Behold this heart that has loved the world so much."

Sister Margaret Mary reported this vision, but many people thought she was deluded and there was much opposition to the new devotion. In fact, devotion to the Sacred Heart was not officially recognized by the Roman Catholic Church during the eighteenth century. But novenas (nine days of prayer) and processions, and chapels and confraternities dedicated to the Sacred Heart, became popular during this time. The rapid spread of this devotion was the most noticeable development in Roman Catholic piety during the eighteenth century. This seemed to show that reason alone was not enough. People needed some concrete, tangible images in addition to abstract theological grounding in their faith.

7. Besides missionary work in foreign lands, missions were preached in the cities and towns of western Europe. Roman Catholic priests and religious traveled from parish to parish and to remote villages, preaching repentance, teaching catechism, and holding special services.

At this time, mission work was revived among the people of Europe. Among Roman Catholics, parishes would dedicate a few days or a week to special sermons, catechism lessons, and liturgical devotions. This was called a "mission." It helped people keep aware of God's presence and deepened their loyalty to the message of Jesus. Often, a mission brought persons back to the practice of their religion.

Missionaries from many orders took part in this work: Jesuits, Capuchins, Passionists, Redemptorists, and others. They had to travel over poor roads in all sorts of weather. They often preached in very poor areas, where the people had little to offer in the way of food and shelter. And their days were as long and full of hard work as those of the peasants to whom they had come.

A missionary might get up around 4:00 A.M. After an hour of personal prayer, he would go to the local church to hear the Confessions of the people. As morning arrived, he would offer Mass and deliver the first mission sermon of the day. There would be another gathering in church in the afternoon, or in the evening if that was more convenient for the people. In some villages during mission services, most of the people could be found in church. Sermons on the passion and death of Jesus were often the most effective ones in melting people's hearts. Sometimes people would be moved to stand up and tell everyone how they had strayed from God. Sometimes preachers would whip themselves to show that we all must try to make up for our own sins and those of others. Sometimes people would carry heavy crosses during processions as acts of penance.

These actions sometimes led to exaggeration and distortion of what was true and important. But these missions often helped to improve local life in important ways. Committees would be formed to help restore peace among quarreling families and get rid of hatred among neighbors. As a result, families and relatives might make peace after years of argument, or a mother might pardon someone who had killed her son. Local groups would often meet to pray or to help those in great need. When the missionaries left the village, a cross was sometimes planted in the public square to remind the people of the mission and the pledges they had made during it.

8. To help explain this mission work among Roman Catholics, we will read about the lives of two great preachers: Leonard of Port Maurice and Paul of the Cross. Leonard became a Franciscan and spent his life giving missions. He wanted everyone to make peace with God and with other people. Paul, a great spiritual leader and mystic, founded a religious congregation called the Passionists.

The lives of two outstanding preachers of this time can help us to understand better the mission work among Roman Catholics.

Leonard of Port Maurice (1676-1751) was attracted to the religious life at the age of twelve, and he entered the Franciscan Order of the Friars Minor. Over a period of 44 years he preached over 300 missions. In the monastery he was very reserved and quiet, but he became almost a different person when he was out among people. His sermons were a lively call, urging people to return to the house of their heavenly Father. People crowded into the churches where he preached. Leonard would remain at church all night, hearing people's confessions. He wanted everyone to make peace with God and with their neighbors. One time he converted a famous pirate, and a well known bandit. Thousands of people journeyed miles to hear him and ask for his advice. When he was close to death, Leonard wrote: "I would like to die soon, so that I can enjoy God and live in the realm where love is practiced perfectly."

As a young man Paul of the Cross (1694-1775), was not sure what God wanted him to

do. He wished that he had lived in the time of Crusades, so that he could have fought for the Christian faith. But gradually he realized that other sorts of effort and struggle were in store for him. He began to live a life of penance, service, and prayer. This led to a mystical experience around 1721. He now realized what his mission was to be: "Through the mercy of God I now know that I desire no other knowledge or consolation except to be crucified with Jesus." With some companions he began to preach missions to the people, even though other priests and religious opposed him. One witness reports that "his words were like thrusts of a sword." A bandit reported that he began to tremble when he saw Paul go up into the pulpit to preach.

Paul founded a religious congregation of priests known as the Passionist Fathers. They were to live in imitation of Jesus's own passion. Through intense prayer and solitary meditation, they were to learn the lessons of Jesus' passion and preach them to the people.

Paul is regarded as one of the great Italian mystics and spiritual leaders of the Roman Catholic Church during the eighteenth century.

9. Sincere and dedicated
   scholars looking for truth
   tried to bring the light
   of reason and historical
   honesty to learning.
   In Italy, Muratori
   explored his country's
   history and discovered
   an important list
   of New Testament books
   which had been accepted
   by the early Church.

Many thinkers of the Enlightenment (or Age of Reason) rejected church institutions and revealed religion even though many of these people still believed in God. But there were also thinkers and scholars who contributed much information and research to the Enlightenment without turning away from their Church.

One such scholar was Ludovico Muratori (1672-1750), an Italian priest of great learning who became one of the finest scholars of his time. A parish priest and the librarian for the duke of Modena, he published many large volumes of historical source material. Many of these books are still important as records of the history of Italy in the Middle Ages. He also discovered the *Muratorian Canon*, which contained the earliest known list of New Testament books and which dated back to A.D. 190.

Muratori also wanted to reform church life. He urged that the number of feast days with Mass obligation be reduced, that legendary and superstitious practices be done away with, and that Roman Catholics be better informed about the Church's liturgy. People such as Muratori were Roman Catholic advocates of true scholarly and historical "enlightenment." In Italy, France, and elsewhere they helped to reconcile new trends with the old faith. But there was opposition, too, from those who felt traditional religious beliefs should not be given up.

In northern Germany, Lutheran theology became strong again during this period. And scholarly concern, emphasis on reason, and religious devotion combined in the work of many German writers and thinkers. This can be seen, for example, in the works of Gotthold Lessing, an influential German thinker and writer. Lessing furthered the ideals of the German version of the Enlightenment, which preserved belief in God but rejected formal Christianity.

A Roman Catholic counterpart of Muratori in Germany was John Michael Sailer (1754-1832). The son of a poor cobbler, he became a priest and taught moral and pastoral theology in various German universities. He wrote many books and he was also a fine preacher. He had the ability to make difficult truths clear to people, and he convinced many wavering Catholics to remain in the Church. He was not afraid to carry on discussions with Protestants, and he maintained good relations with many of them. He tried to stress the points on which Roman Catholics and Protestants agreed.

10.
To help explain life in Spain in the 1700s, we will read the story of Miguel, an imaginary young Spaniard. At this time, Spain was more united as a country than in the past, but it was becoming poorer. Miguel was the oldest son in an aristocratic family that was no longer rich.

Miguel, the imaginary young man in our story of eighteenth-century Spain, was the firstborn son in an aristocratic family. His family had once been extremely wealthy, but now it had lost some of its money. This was the case with many of the old Spanish families, for Spain had become a poorer country.

Miguel's father thought he had found the way to improve his family's fortune: He planned for Miguel to marry the daughter of a rich merchant. The bride-to-be would bring a very rich dowry to her husband. (A dowry was a gift of money and land from the bride's family.) The merchant's family would also benefit by the marriage because they would now be related to the aristocracy.

Like the typical Spaniard of his time, Miguel was loyal to the Roman Catholic Church. Moreover, he was greatly attracted by the renewed spirit of religious devotion in the Church.

After much thought, Miguel told his astonished and unhappy father that he did not intend to marry. Instead, he planned to give his life to the service of the Church as a Franciscan friar.

Miguel's father coaxed him to change his mind and then he threatened to punish Miguel with beatings and imprisonment. But both coaxing and threatening failed. Then the old lord suggested that Miguel become a diocesan priest instead of a friar in an order. Because he was an aristocrat, Miguel would certainly become at least a bishop if he was ordained as a diocesan priest. This was the case with many sons of aristocratic families who entered the priesthood.

Other family members joined the lord in pleading with Miguel. If he became a Franciscan, they said, he would work among the common people, who were coarse and ignorant and often dirty. That was not the life for a nobleman, they told him. Even if he didn't want to become a diocesan priest, he should not become a wandering, begging friar. Instead, he should join a monastery. There he could live a quiet life of prayer away from the world.

And of course some relatives thought Miguel's whole idea was silly because they thought little about God, religion, or the Church.

Miguel took it all in silently and sadly, but he did not change his mind. He was determined to dedicate his life to the service of the Church and the needy people in Spain. He went to the nearby Franciscan monastery and began his life as a novice in the Franciscan order.

11. We continue our story of Miguel, an imaginary Spaniard of the 1700s. Miguel became a Franciscan friar and went to live in a fishing village on the coast of Galicia. There he became the spiritual leader of his parish and helped his people in many ways.

There were many priests and religious in Spain, but most of them lived in the big cities. The cathedrals and wealthier parishes were located there. The comfortable monasteries and convents of religious orders, the regional universities and seminaries were also in the cities. Church life in such surroundings was considered an honorable career for daughters and sons of the aristocratic families. But not many an oldest son—the chief heir—entered church service, as did our imaginary Miguel.

When Miguel had finished his novitiate, he was officially received into the Franciscan order. Then his superior discussed with him his future work. He suggested that Miguel go to the city and live in a Franciscan house while he took courses in philosophy, theology, and canon law at the university. In this way he could prepare for an important career. He might become the close adviser of some bishop. Or he might serve on some important church tribunal (court).

Miguel was not interested in such offers. He had no desire to earn an advanced degree in theology, which seemed to him rather cold and boring. Neither did he want to become an important or powerful person in the political life of the Church. He wanted to dedicate his life to preaching the Christian message and teaching the faith. He knew that there were many loyal

Catholics outside the big cities who had few priests to teach them. Miguel wanted to serve the Church in such a place.

So Miguel was sent to a rural fishing village on the Atlantic coast in a region known as Galicia. No priest had lived in the village for many years, although traveling Franciscans had visited the villagers from time to time. Now the people there would have a full-time spiritual leader.

Miguel found that the spiritual life of the fishing village was surprisingly alive and strong. There were sacramental ceremonies for all the major events in life, novenas (nine days of prayer) at different times of the year, and meetings of the villagers for prayer at certain other times.

Religious confraternities still played an important role in village life. All the fishermen of the village belonged to a confraternity dedicated to Mary the Mother of Jesus under the title Our Lady of Help. They called on her to protect them from the dangers of life at sea. When they arrived home safely from a fishing trip, the confraternity would celebrate with religious processions, festive meals, and joyous parties.

Miguel enjoyed living with these people. He shared in their joys and sorrows, bringing them the message of Jesus Christ.

12. Our story of Miguel ends with a description of his efforts to help his people during a time of crop failure and famine.

During the life time of our imaginary Spaniard, Miguel, the Roman Catholic Church in Spain was quite wealthy. Besides its income in money from tithes and contributions, its dioceses, cathedrals, and religious orders owned much land.

Some Spaniards were beginning to say that this church land should be taken over by private individuals who would use their money to improve the land and produce more crops. Even though now the Church made charitable donations to help the needy, it would be better, these Spaniards said, if the people could grow more food themselves.

Such reasoning might make sense, but—as Miguel found out—poor people often need the Church to help them handle immediate problems. Their lives were harsh and difficult. When bad weather, famine, plague, and drought endangered their lives, it was often only the Church that came to their aid. So people had come to feel that the Church should have resources on hand to help the common people in times of trouble.

Miguel's villagers now faced such a time of trouble. They had a poor fishing season, and then a heavy rain destroyed their crops. There was no way to replenish their food supply, and they faced starvation.

Under Miguel's leadership, a group left the village to go to the city of Santiago de Compostella. In this city there was a shrine to St. James the apostle. The archbishop and the priests of the cathedral there distributed food daily to the needy.

In Santiago de Compostella, the travelers from Galicia were given shelter in local monasteries. Food, clothing, and money were gathered for them. Miguel took part in this charitable work.

Some days later, the group set off for their home again, carrying bundles of food and clothing and driving a cart piled with grain and other things the village needed.

As Miguel walked among the happy villagers and joined in their hymns of praise and thanks, he remembered the aristocratic home of his boyhood. And Miguel was very happy to be where he was now.

13. In the early 1700s, most European countries were ruled by monarchs through the agreements they made with wealthy merchants and with the nobility. Church officials also had high positions. Later, this way of ruling was called the Old Regime.

In the early 1700s most parts of Europe, as well as the French and Spanish colonies in America, were ruled under a system known as the *Ancien Régime*. The two French words mean the "Old Regime." (A regime is a system.) It was in France that the system was first developed in its most complete form. Other countries, with the exception of England, imitated the French model.

The Old Regime was a system with many medieval features. It kept many of the ancient laws and constitutions. There were still many large landowners who could force work out of peasants on their lands and make legal decisions in court cases. But in some ways the Old Regime was new. It depended on overseas commerce. It was a highly organized government, with a king or prince at its head who had supreme power. The Old Regime did not have representative bodies such as the assemblies of feudal lords and free peasants of the Middle Ages, the merchant councils of the Middle Ages and the Renaissance, or the parliaments of the nineteenth century. Instead it could rule because of a close alliance between wealthy merchants, high noblemen, the ruler, and the ruler's government officials.

Peasants and craftsmen were the productive workers. They formed the economic basis of society. But they had little say in the world of the ruling classes and the mighty. The latter included wealthy merchants, bankers, government officials, and high churchmen. These people either formed part of the nobility or were seeking to enter it. Wealth, power, a good marriage, and good connections were some of the keys to success. Members of the nobility, including churchmen, enjoyed benefits and freedoms that the common people did not enjoy.

The world of the Old Regime might seem elegant, glittering, formal, and highly cultured. But underneath there was much conflict, violence, and ill feeling. Many people tried to win favor and power from the ruler, to get more and more for themselves and their families. The burden of paying for all this fell on the shoulders of the unprivileged classes. Their situation would improve during the eighteenth century, leading to hopes that would encourage them to demand a fairer share of power and influence. And these hopes and demands would lead to the revolutions of the eighteenth and nineteenth centuries.

The French Revolution in 1789 marked the end of the "old regime" and the birth of the "new regime" not only in France but in most of Europe.

14. Freemasonry began to spread in England and Europe in the 1700s. Masonic meetings were held in secret and involved rituals and discussions of philosophy and religion.

During the eighteenth century, many groups were formed by people who wanted to discuss their ideas with others who had the same view of the world, life, and religion. Freemasonry is an example of one such successful group. Masonry had arisen at a much earlier time, though exactly when is not known for sure. It may go back to the medieval stonemasons, who formed corporations for common prayer and mutual help.

When Masonry showed up in England around 1650, the type of people in the group and their activities had changed. Instead of workers, most of the members were noblemen or middle-class people. Masonic meetings involved secrets and discussions of a philosophical and religious nature. A group of Masons in a particular place was called a lodge. Members were divided into apprentices, companions, and masters. Their symbols were the stonemason's tools: the plumb, the square, the level, and the compass.

England was the intellectual home of the Enlightenment, and it was there that modern Masonry first flourished. Masons put Enlightenment principles into practice. Masons were ethical in the way that the Enlightenment was

ethical; that is, they wanted to do what was right and what would help other people, but they denied Christian revelation and principles. Masons believed in God as creator, but they believed that after creation, God no longer took active part in creation's development. And Masons did not believe that people were called to a supernatural life.

A grand lodge of Freemasonry was formed in England in 1717. The movement began to grow in England and on the continent of Europe. The complicated rituals and the air of secrecy surrounding Masonic meetings seemed to appeal to certain people. They felt that a small group of people with good will and enlightened ideas might arrive at some great truth that would benefit the world.

Many Roman Catholic churchmen belonged to Masonic lodges. It is estimated that in 1789, just before the outbreak of the French Revolution, about one-fourth of the Masons in France were churchmen. Many of the leaders of the American Revolution were members of Masonic lodges.

In some countries, such as in the United States, Masonry did not strongly compete with religion. But in some other countries and especially in the eighteenth century, Masons were openly hostile to organized Christianity.

The Society of Jesus strongly opposed Freemasonry and prohibited its members from becoming Masons. In 1738, Pope Clement XII condemned Masonry and forbade Roman Catholics to join the Masons. This ban is still in force.

15. Early in the eighteenth century, a small group of people interested in spiritual growth gathered under John Wesley. He developed a method to help them progress in spiritual life. This was the beginning of the Methodist Church.

In the 1700s, John Wesley (1703-1791) began a powerful reform movement within the Anglican Church. As a young man, Wesley was dissatisfied with Anglicanism. He felt that there was little sense of personal religious experience in Anglican worship and that the Church did not do enough to help the lower classes grow spiritually. Also, Wesley saw that the Enlightenment was weakening the Anglican Church.

As a young deacon at Oxford University, Wesley gathered a small group of friends around him and worked out a method of making spiritual progress. It involved prayer, spiritual readings, fasts, and works of charity. Because of this "method," the people involved came to be called Methodists.

In 1735 Wesley went to the colony of Georgia in America as an Anglican missionary. There he insisted on strict observance of Anglican ritual and preached against the slave trade and liquor. He met with angry resistance and had to flee back to England. There he began to take part in the religious worship of the Moravian Brotherhood, a Protestant religious faith. While reading Martin Luther's commentary on Paul's letter to the Romans. Wesley underwent a deep and moving personal experience. He suddenly felt certain that

Christ had indeed saved him and that he could put all his trust in Christ.

John Wesley devoted his life to bringing this conviction to others. At first he tried to preach in Anglican Churches. The congregations did not like his enthusiastic approach, nor did they like his inviting lowly workers and seedy characters to his sermons.

Wesley began to preach in the open air in 1739 and thousands began to show up. Many people were deeply moved by his sermons, and they were also helped to have a concrete personal experience of prayer, mutual help, and charity. Wesley emphasized the importance of Christ's saving work rather than predestination.

Methodism grew, and in 1744 the first general conference of Methodists took place. Slowly Methodism began to separate from the Anglican Church. After 1776, when the United States became an independent nation, Methodist priests were needed there. Anglican bishops refused to ordain Methodists, and so Wesley himself ordained Methodist clerics and sent them to the United States. John Wesley never broke away from the Anglican Church explicitly, but his followers took that step soon after the death of their tireless, energetic, and inspiring leader.

16. Pietism, like Methodism, was a reform movement. It emphasized religious feelings and practices. Pietism influenced both religion and culture, as is shown in the life and work of Zinzendorf and the music of Bach.

In the 1600s, an important religious movement called Pietism was started in Germany for the purpose of bringing new life into the Protestant religion. Pietism emphasized religious feelings and practices rather than encouraging re-examination of church dogmas. It wished to encourage the growth of faith and love in the hearts of the faithful. Like Methodism, Pietism was a reaction against the Enlightenment's emphasis on natural laws.

During the 1700s, Pietism continued to influence Germany. One example of this is seen in the life of Count Nicholas of Zinzendorf (1700-1760), a dedicated Pietist. He established the small village of Herrnhut (The Lord's Care) on his estates, where persecuted members of the Moravian Brethren and of other religious sects could live in safety. A central belief of all the inhabitants of Herrnhut was that the blood of Christ had redeemed humanity. The Herrnhuters showed love and tenderness for each other and love for God and trust in him.

Zinzendorf's support of the Herrnhuters strengthened the missionary work of the Moravian Brethren. Later, it had a strong influence on the Lutheran Church itself.

Pietism also influenced German culture, especially in music. Religious feeling in the eighteenth century found powerful expression in the works of Johann Sebastian Bach (1685-1750), one of the greatest European composers. Bach lived and died a relatively unknown man; much of his musical work was not published during his lifetime. He was truly ecumenical as a composer of religious music. For example, though he was a Lutheran he composed Roman Catholic Masses for the Elector of Saxony. Bach's work is now known and played throughout the world.

17. Four important people of the French Enlightenment are Montesquieu, Voltaire, Rousseau, and Diderot. They tried to bring the light of reason to many areas of life, including government, history, attitudes toward other cultures, education, and religion. Their works were widely read.

French-speaking thinkers and writers played an important role in the Enlightenment. They were impressed by English thinkers and scientists, particularly by John Locke and Isaac Newton. They were also impressed by the English form of government and its seeming tolerance of various religious groups. Certain French thinkers tried to bring the light of reason to various areas of life in their own country. This group of writer/philosophers came to be known as the *philosophes*. Their varied and wide-ranging writings were read in many different countries. We will mention only four of them.

The Baron of Montesquieu (1689-1755) helped to form the general atmosphere of the Enlightenment with his *Persian Letters* (1721). These were a series of imaginary letters written by or to Persian travellers to Europe. Through the remarks in these imaginary letters, Montesquieu amusingly criticized French habits and institutions that looked silly when examined by reasonable human beings. His later work, *The Spirit of Laws* (1750), was a pioneering study of various forms of government and the attitudes of people living under them. This important work had an influence on the framing of the United States Constitution.

Probably the most versatile and lively of the *philosophes* of the French Enlightenment was François Marie Arouet (1694-1778), who came to be known as Voltaire. He was one of the first men of letters to earn fame and wealth in a writing career. He wrote almost every kind of work: history and biography; plans, stories, and sketches; popular travel reports and scholarly articles. Educated by the Jesuits, Voltaire was—in his own way—a sincere moralist. He hated war, social injustice, religious intolerance, and unreasonable forms of authority. Anything blocking human reasoning and freedom might be fair game for his biting, witty attacks. He looked on religion as superstition and religious authority as tyranny because he believed that Christianity was a lie. He wanted to destroy the Christian religion. Nevertheless, Voltaire believed in a God and continued to write to one of his old clerical teachers.

Another major figure was a Genevan by birth: Jean Jacques Rousseau (1712-1778). Rousseau saw violence growing with the rise of civilization, and he wanted society to be less artificial and complicated. He exalted and romanticized earlier and simpler ways of life, yet did not believe that people should return to the primitive state. He believed that the heart was a better judge of right thinking and virtuous living than reason was, but he also felt that there was a place for religion and the fine teachings of the Gospels.

Denis Diderot (1713-1784) was the creative editor and guiding hand behind the remarkable French *Encyclopedia*. Seventeen volumes of text and eleven volumes of picture plates were published between 1751 and 1772. The aim of the *Encyclopedia* was reform as well as knowledge: "To assemble the knowledge scattered over the earth, to explain its general outline to those with whom we live, and to transmit it to those who come after us...so that our descendants, by becoming better informed, may therefore be happier and more virtuous." (The *Encyclopaedia Britannica* an English-language work was also published for the first time in three volumes between 1768 and 1771.)

The *philosophes* felt that they had shed some light on human life during their century. When the American Revolution succeeded and the government of the United States was formed, they felt that the Enlightenment had been a success because many of the Enlightenment's ideals of human freedom were furthered by the new nation.

18. Benedict XIV, who became
pope in 1740, brought
great understanding and
respect for other people's
ideas to his work. He was
also a humble person
of great learning, and
he had a sense of humor.
Under his leadership,
the Church emphasized
its great concern
for the care of souls.

Pope Benedict XIV (reigned 1740-1758) chose not to focus on the matters of papal authority and political rights which had concerned the popes just before him. Instead he turned to religious and pastoral concerns. Benedict XIV was a friend of Leonard of Port Maurice, Ludovico Muratori, and other dedicated men of religion. He combined great learning and wisdom with an obvious humility. All this was mixed with an appealing sense of humor.

Benedict XIV restored the old practice of washing the feet of poor people during the service on Holy Thursday in imitation of Jesus' action at the Last Supper. He drew up plans for revising the liturgical books of the Church and the list of obligatory feasts. He also wanted to revise the Index of forbidden books, a list of books which Roman Catholics were not allowed to read without special permission. In revising this list, Benedict XIV was especially anxious that the books get a fair reading and not be unjustly placed on the list.

In dealing with other people, Benedict was able to put himself in their place and to understand their ideas and feelings. He tried to see what was good in their point of view. Throughout his life, Benedict tried to maintain good relations with people who looked on the Church unfavorably. He even exchanged letters with Voltaire, who had a high regard for Benedict. However, the pope fully realized the danger for the Church if Catholics became divided about correct morality. He knew that the Catholic Church had to be defended against those who sought to weaken it.

Benedict XIV was pope during a period of political conflicts, and the papal territory (land in Italy ruled by the pope) became a battleground between Spanish and Austrian troops in 1740. The pope protested strongly, but his basic approach was to reconcile the parties involved.

Benedict XIV remained energetic and lively to a ripe old age. He did much to enrich the library and various museums of the Vatican. He himself was a learned expert in theology and canon law, and he helped to make Rome a center of cultural life especially by the support he gave to building up the collections in the Vatican Museum.

19. Enemies of the Jesuits among ruling families and some lay people successfully pressured the pope to suppress the Jesuit order in 1773.

The Society of Jesus, founded by Ignatius of Loyola, had become an active and important order in the life of the Church. The Jesuits were busy in foreign missions, home missions, and schools. They had created many schools of high quality in which some of the brightest and most talented people of Europe were educated.

To make society truly Christian and Roman Catholic, the Jesuits often chose to deal with important people. They often served as confessors to rulers, or as trusted advisers at the king's court. This aroused the envy of other people at court, and it also involved the Jesuits in political disputes. Many defenders of absolute kingly power did not trust the Jesuits, since they vowed obedience only to their own Superiors and the pope. Royal officials felt that the Church should be subject to the State, and they disliked the Church's ties with the papacy in Rome. Moreover, the Jesuits sometimes were so concerned about teaching influential people that they forgot one of their original aims: to teach simple people.

At this time, many people tended to rely on human reason and sense experience, and they did not care for supernatural mysteries and dogmatic beliefs. They had little respect for the contemplative life of religious orders or for the educational work of an authoritative Church based in Rome. While religious orders who were engaged in works of charity might be acceptable to them, those which did not engage in socially useful activities seemed to be useless.

In Portugal, where there was tension between the Church and the government, the Marquis of Pombal succeeded in getting the Jesuits expelled from the country. The same thing happened in Spain, the Kingdom of Naples, and the Duchies of Parma and Piacenza, regions ruled by members of the Bourbon family. Jesuits were expelled from France in 1764.

In 1773, under pressure from opponents of the Jesuits, Pope Clement XIV signed a document which ordered that the Society of Jesus be disbanded. Some Jesuits became secular priests, and some fled to non-Catholic countries, such as Prussia and Russia.

Clement had hoped that suppressing the Jesuits' would improve relations between the Roman Catholic Church and the Bourbon rulers, but it did not. But the Church was hurt because missions and schools were closed down, and other Jesuit works simply stopped.

20. English and German thinkers of the Enlightenment wrote important works about new theories of education and religion.

From the middle of the seventeenth century on, important original thinking was going on in England and Scotland. Some thinkers involved in this work stressed the importance of observation and experience in gathering knowledge. They believed that knowledge is not already present in the human mind at birth but that we have to gather data (facts) in order to be able to think about things and make up theories.

John Locke (1632-1704) described the human mind as a clean slate (*tabula rasa*) at birth. Life and its experiences, he believed, fill the slate with information. (Today the *tabula rasa* theory is rejected by scholars.)

Locke was one of the leading English thinkers in the Enlightenment, or Age of Reason. He described society as the result of a contract between free and equal individuals, and he urged a system of checks and balances between various branches of government. In his essay *On the Reasonableness of Christianity* (1696), Locke emphasized ethical principles over dogma; that is, he felt right living was more important than abstract truths about God. Locke retained belief in the divinity of Christ and the practical usefulness of scripture.

Locke wrote about education, government, and religion in a clear, commonsense way. There were problems buried in the ideas he presented so very persuasively, but it took sharp, critical minds to see them. For example, Voltaire felt that Locke's version of Christianity was really a new religion. Many churchmen felt the same way.

David Hume (1711-1776), Scottish philosopher and historian, had perhaps the sharpest philosophical mind among Enlightenment figures in English-speaking lands. He, too, was a fine, clear writer who dealt with many subjects. But some of his conclusions about religious and philosophical issues were extreme and drastic. Hume wrote that human beings should put reason to the fullest possible use, but that it did have limits. Indeed, in the end, reason should be the servant of the passions and should aim only "to serve and obey them."

Hume believed that our minds were a bundle of sense impressions and that conclusions we reach about our world and life should be based on reason or provable argument rather than on religious belief.

Towards the end of the seventeenth century, people in German-speaking lands began to show great intellectual liveliness. The University of Halle was founded in 1694, to be followed later by important universities in Göttingen and Berlin. The great philosopher Gottfried Wilhelm Leibniz (1646-1716) was eager to find some way of reconciling divine realities with the ongoing struggle of human thought and life. His wide-ranging work was not really known and appreciated during the Enlightenment period, but it is now being rediscovered, explored, and appreciated.

Another great German thinker, Immanual Kant (1724-1804) saw the Age of Reason as the change of human beings from childhood to adulthood. People must have the courage to think for themselves, to use reason correctly, Kant believed. This would help them acquire knowledge and lead to a better, more peaceful world. For Kant, religion was simply a matter of seeing duty as a command from God. Conscience told people all they needed to know, and divine revelation, even a personal redeemer like Jesus, was unnecessary and really impossible.

21. New scientific theories (such as Newton's laws of motion and gravitation) and important inventions (such as the steam engine) changed people's attitudes and way of life.

New theories and experiments in science and technology that had been developed in the seventeenth century became widely known and accepted in the eighteenth. The findings of small scientific societies were now studied and admired by noblemen and other educated people, and new thinking in other areas of life as well was also encouraged.

Isaac Newton (1642-1721) worked out his laws about motion and gravitation and published a report in 1687. His work offered a new and clear picture of the universe to thinking people. Newton himself sincerely believed in God. But when people who read his works began to study the visible universe, some of them began to think of the universe as a well-made machine. To them, God was a great

"clockmaker" who had built the clock (the universe), wound it up, and then pretty much left it to run for itself. And they found the clock so interesting in itself that they forgot about God the clockmaker; he seemed far off in his heavens and not much interested in his creation. This basic outlook was shared by such thinkers as Descartes and Leibniz.

In the eighteenth century no important new scientific theory was formulated, but some important discoveries were made. Oxygen was discovered, and people tried to figure out what electricity was and how it worked. People also tried to understand the relationship between heat and energy (thermodynamics). Scientists began to try to build more precise measuring tools and instruments in order to have more control over their experiments. The number of new inventions grew as the century went on.

In 1733 John Kay invented an automatic fly shuttle which speeded up the weaving of cloth. Soon after that, other inventions further improved weaving and spinning. James Watt (1736-1819) repaired and improved an earlier model of the steam engine. His new type of engine was important in the Industrial Revolution, which was under way in England before the end of the eighteenth century. In this revolution, the increased use of iron as a building material—such as in bridges—and of steam as a source of power would be very important.

Canada

22. Scotland and England joined in 1707 to form Great Britain, which became the most powerful country in Europe. It ruled Ireland and owned thirteen English colonies in North America. To this, Britain added Canada, which it had won from France in war. England was largely Anglican in religion but, in Canada and Ireland, Roman Catholics were the majority.

In England, the Anglican Church (Church of England) had settled down to a quiet period around 1690. There was little theological dispute until John Wesley began Methodism (1739). Roman Catholics in England were an insignificant minority. Deprived of political rights, many Catholics lived in rural areas near the homes of gentlemen still loyal to the Roman Catholic Church. Usually a chaplain lived on the gentleman's estate and provided Catholic sacraments. Around the end of the 1700s, political hostility to Roman Catholics began to lessen in England. Roman Catholics in Scotland also suffered greatly, and some of them went to North America. There they settled in Nova Scotia (New Scotland).

The English ruled the Roman Catholics of Ireland with an iron hand. Even though Roman Catholics there were the overwhelming majority, they were not allowed to take part in public life. Goods and farmlands were taken away from native Irish Catholics. Men and women of religious orders were expelled from the country, and strict controls were placed over priests. For Irish Catholics, the English rule was a time of persecution, but no such persecution was visited on the Protestants who lived in the northern part of Ireland (present-day Ulster plus two other counties).

Some changes began to take place in the Catholic parts of Ireland during the eighteenth century. In 1782 permission was given to build churches, and religious freedom came in 1790. In 1795, the national seminary of Maynooth was opened.

Great Britain
and
Ireland

Dublin

London

The religious situation in the colony of Canada was different. While Canada had been a French possession, Roman Catholicism had taken root and spread. Jesuits, Franciscans, and Capuchins had worked there. In the central city of Quebec, Mother d'Youville had established the Sisters of Charity in 1737. When Canada was conquered by Great Britain, the English hoped to spread Anglicanism and transform Quebec into a Protestant city. But Canadian Catholics resisted, and in 1774 King George III had to restore freedom of worship and respect French customs. Archbishop Plessis of Quebec, the first to hold that office, provided important leadership to the Roman Catholic Church in Quebec.

Sans-Souci

Versailles

Madrid

Schoenbrunn

Caserta

23.
Under the influence of the Enlightenment, a form of government arose called "enlightened despotism."

During the Enlightenment period there was new interest in political and social life, greater stress on human reason, and growing appeals to foster human welfare and happiness. People felt that their living conditions could and should be improved. These same thoughts and feelings were probably shared by many rulers, though they may have felt that the proper way to do such things was to strengthen their own power as heads of government. (A visible sign of this power was the grand palaces of the rulers, some of which are shown on this map.) Many rulers claimed that they were influenced by the French *philosophes* (thinkers of the French Enlightenment) as they tried to strengthen their own control by governmental reforms. Their approach has been called "enlightened despotism."

Real changes and reforms were made, but in most cases rule by kings and princes became stronger and more absolute. Rulers wanted to see an increase in production of goods and in population. So measures were passed to improve agriculture, to open new farmlands with the help of pioneers, and to welcome settlers from other parts of Europe. New crops, the potato in particular, were cultivated because they greatly increased the available food supply. Rulers also wanted to make their government more efficient. For example, some rulers and their ministers also began to pay closer attention to the income and expenses of the government. Hence efforts were made to improve the collection of taxes and other sources of money. In short, many aspects of the government's approach were changed in order to make it easier for rulers to establish their authority right down to the level of the individual in a distant village. As a result, government bureaucracy came forward as a major factor in people's lives.

This process of reform and centralization of power did not work out successfully everywhere. But it was helped along in many places by the real need for reform which dedicated people saw. Service to the government seemed to be a noble ideal to various people and groups.

24. In Russia, Peter the Great organized his empire so that he had absolute authority over everything and everyone. He built a new capital city named St. Petersburg (today called Leningrad). His work was continued by Catherine the Great. Peter and Catherine wanted the Russian Church to be under the czar's control. The office of Patriarch (head of the Church) was done away with.

In the eighteenth century important changes took place in Russia, which now began to step forward on the stage of European history. Czar Peter the Great (reigned 1682-1725) played a very important part in this whole process. The czar became an absolute ruler, even over the nobility. Noblemen were to render service to the state in military and civilian jobs. They had to obey the czar, who could promote or demote them. Peter was much impressed with western Europe and wanted Russia to borrow whatever would help it make progress. He reorganized the army, improved the tax system, encouraged trade, and tried to encourage the manufacture of goods. On the southern shore of the Baltic Sea on territory recently won back from Sweden, Peter had a new city built at great cost. He called it St. Petersburg (after himself) and made it the new capital of Russia.

This work of strengthening the power of the czar was extended by Catherine II (reigned 1762-1796), who is also known as Catherine the Great. She maintained contact with French *philosophes* such as Diderot and Voltaire and claimed to be a follower of their ideas, though it is doubtful that her sort of dictatorial rule was what the *philosophes* really had in mind. But during Catherine's rule, Russians did begin to take more notice of what was going on in western Europe.

Peter the Great had an important influence

on the Russian Orthodox Church. He seemed to prefer Ukrainian and Protestant clergymen to Orthodox clergy; he had felt that Russian Orthodoxy was too contemplative and passive and too much influenced by its clergy. Peter wanted the Russian Orthodox Church to be completely under the control of the Russian emperor. The Ecclesiastical Regulation of 1721 imposed his will on the Russian Church. The office of patriarch (head of the Russian Church) was abolished. A Holy Synod was established as a formal government department of religion. The Russian Church lost its independence and became a branch of the government.

Both Peter and Catherine did not care much for monks and monasteries. They saw monasticism as a useless way of life. But their hostile views did not destroy the influence of monasticism in Russia, where people admired and respected monks and their monasteries.

25. In 1763, a German bishop in a book written under the pen name of Febronius discussed papal authority. Febronius believed that the pope's power did not extend over other bishops. A little later, Emperor Joseph II, an enlightened despot, tried to gain control of the Roman Catholic Church in his lands.

As attempts were being made to organize government more efficiently, some Roman Catholics began to feel that the Church should be more subject to national control and less tied to the authority of the pope in Rome. This idea was widely held in German-speaking lands, where a power struggle was going on among people of power and influence.

In 1763 Bishop von Hontheim published a book under the pen name of Febronius. It was entitled *Concerning the Condition of the Church and the Legitimate Power of the Pope.* Febronius wanted a return to the simple life of the early Church. He maintained that the pope's position of primacy (being first among the bishops) was only an honor and did not give him ruling power over other bishops. In a country where the Church was established, Febronius wrote, authority over the Church should be in the hands of its national bishops. Also, Febronius believed that the pope was not infallible and that the bishops' disagreement with the pope's decisions should be submitted to a General Council of the Church. Febronius also declared that a ruler had a

right to carry out church reforms and to oppose excessive interference by the pope.

Febronius's book was condemned by the pope, and the author took back some of what he had written. His book was very popular, even in Catholic circles, and was widely read. His ideas were called Febronianism.

A wave of church reforms flooded the Hapsburg lands when Joseph II (reigned 1780-1790) became emperor. His approach came to be known as Josephism. He was a religious man and was also an "enlightened despot." Joseph planned to make government serve reason, and his programs dealt with almost every area of life. There was to be greater freedom, fairer taxes, and more land ownership for peasants. School was to be compulsory and more practical. Censorship was abolished, practices Joseph considered superstitious were criticized, and greater freedom for some Protestant denominations was permitted. Catholic clergy were forbidden to write directly to Rome, and papal decrees could not be put into force in the emperor's territory without his approval. Joseph reorganized parishes and seminaries and greatly reduced the number of convents.

Joseph failed to persuade his subjects that his reforms were the right thing to do, and there was much resentment against his measures. All of his reforms collapsed soon after his death, when a hostile reaction set in.

26. The British colonies
in North America grew
and prospered during the
eighteenth century.
More and more European
immigrants arrived
at eastern ports and
moved inland to cultivate
farms. The first Christian
communities in the British
colonies were mostly
Protestant.

By the middle of the eighteenth century there were three major zones of influence in the Americas. In Latin America, extending from Mexico through South America, Spanish and Portuguese influence prevailed. In Canada, the settlers were mostly French and English. In what is now the Eastern part of the United States, British influence ruled.

The British colonies were growing, attracting an increasing number of European immigrants. English laborers, Irish farmhands, and Scottish and German settlers left their homelands, looking for better living conditions. The first steps in the journey were difficult. They had to save the money for the trip, then board ship at some port in Ireland, England, or even Holland. Those without money had to pledge

to work without pay in the New World for three, four, or five years, if their patron or landland would pay their travel fees for them.

After the new settlers had arrived and had paid off their debts, they often moved inland to find their own farmlands. They had to cut down trees and clear land to use as fields for planting. They had to find water and fodder for their animals.

The settlers often chose to live in groups in order to have protection from outlaws and hostile Indians. In most cases the groups were formed on the basis of people's home country and religion. English settlers tended to be Anglicans or Puritans. The Scots were Calvinists. Most of the early Irish settlers were Scotch Irish, from northern Ireland, and were Protestant. The German settlers were usually Lutheran.

Religious differences were obvious in community life. The Calvinists, some of whom were Puritans and Presbyterians, gathered to hear the Bible read by an elder. Roman Catholics, a very small minority, met in small groups for the Mass and other Roman Catholic devotions.

Often, after clearing their land and paying for it, colonists resold it and moved on to break new ground elsewhere, continually pushing the frontier forward. Less adventurous immigrants came behind them to occupy and enjoy lands already won.

27. In 1776, Great Britain's American colonies became independent and formed a new country—the United States of America. In its Constitution, the new nation recognized religious freedom. John Carroll became the first American Catholic bishop. The Church of England in the United States became the Protestant Episcopal Church.

Increased trade, the ongoing colonization of new lands, and greater prosperity in the British American colonies made the colonists more aware of their own importance. They grew increasingly angry about taxes and trade restrictions imposed on them by England. Relations between England and the colonies became so bad that in 1775 war broke out between the Mother Country and the American colonies. This war is known as the American Revolution, or the American War of Independence.

In 1776, a year after the war began, representatives of the thirteen English colonies signed the Declaration of Independence. This document declared that the thirteen colonies were a free and independent country. Thus, it marked the birth of the United States and was an important formulation of the rights of human beings. The declaration affirmed that people are created equal and that God gives all people the right to life, liberty, and the pursuit of happiness.

The American Constitution recognized freedom of religion and equality among all the religious communities in the country. This provision was of great importance to minority religions, such as Roman Catholics. They set about organizing their church and its hierarchy (bishops). On November 6, 1789, John

Carroll was named the first United States' Catholic bishop. He was placed in charge of the diocese (region) of Baltimore, Maryland, which had the largest Catholic population of any state. At that time there were about 25,000 Catholics in a population of some 3,000,000.

The choice of Bishop Carroll was a very good one. He was open and alert to the demands of the new situation. He was also the cousin of one of the signers of the Declaration of Independence, Charles Carroll of Carrollton.

Bishop Carroll went right to work. In 1791 he founded the first Catholic college in America (today, Georgetown University), which he later entrusted to the Jesuits. The following year, with the help of some French priests, Bishop Carroll established a seminary for the training of future priests. When John Carroll died in 1815, there were about 150,000 Catholics and 100 priests in the United States.

By that time there were four dioceses: Baltimore, Boston, Philadelphia, and New York.

Citizens of the newly-formed United States who were members of the Church of England remained within their Church but organized it under a new title: The Protestant Episcopal Church of the United States. Its first American bishop, Samuel Seabury, was consecrated in Scotland in 1784, and a few years later three more American bishops were consecrated in England. Thus the Protestant Episcopal Church came into being as a self-governing church, and in 1789 it produced its own revised edition of *The Book of Common Prayer.*

28. The rule of Grand Duke Leopold of Tuscany is an example of "enlightened despotism." Leopold wanted to reform economic life in Tuscany. And he wanted to reform the Church under the leadership of his friend, Bishop Ricci. But the bishop's reforms, which were influenced by Jansenistic views, were rejected by many people, and in 1794 they were condemned by the pope.

An example of "enlightened despotism" in action and of its attack on the central power of the pope is seen in the rule of Grand Duke Leopold I of Tuscany, Italy. As absolute ruler, Leopold had complete authority over his people. He wished to have a Tuscan Church that would be under his authority, with his friend, Bishop Scipione Ricci of Pistoia and Prato, as spiritual leader.

Leopold ruled with honesty and efficiency. He encouraged economic life, reformed the penal code (laws dealing with crime and punishment), and forced the Roman Catholic Inquisition to leave Tuscany. Leopold also freed the serfs, the lowly peasants who had been much like slaves to their lords.

Bishop Ricci favored Jansenistic thinking, and there was a group of Jansenists in Tuscany, though there were not many in Italy. The bishop hoped to combine fresh ideas of church reform with Jansenistic ideas, such as the belief that people should receive Communion only infrequently, and that the priest should

be strict with people when they went to confession. Bishop Ricci called a church meeting or synod at Pistoia in 1786, attended by priests and bishops of his diocese.

Many decisions were made by this synod, and most of them were liberal. The synod wanted more people to be allowed to take part in church government. Priests were to be freer in their relations with their bishops, and the latter in their relations with the pope. There was to be a fairer distribution of church income among the clergy. Also, the liturgy and church devotions were to be simplified and practices that Bishop Ricci considered superstitious were to be removed.

But during the following years, opposition to the synod's findings came from church leaders and from common people too. Some people were unhappy because their favorite devotions and religious practices were being attacked as useless or superstitious. Many church leaders feared that too much was being reformed too quickly.

The bishops of Tuscany met in 1787 and voted to condemn the statements of the Pistoia synod. And in 1794, Pope Pius VI also condemned it.

In 1790 Leopold's brother, Emperor Joseph II of Austria, died. Leopold left Tuscany to become emperor and most of his reforms disappeared amid the turmoil of revolutionary movements. That same year, Bishop Ricci was removed from his diocese and retired to private life. He returned to the Roman Catholic Church before his death.

Another Italian reformer of this period is Cesare Becarrio (1738-1794). He held several public offices in the Austrian government and urged economic reforms. His essay called *On Crimes and Punishments* (1794) is probably his most famous and important work. In it he spoke against capital punishment (the death sentence) and against the inhuman treatment of criminals which was common at this time. His writings encouraged people who worked for the reform of laws dealing with crime and punishment.

29. The French Revolution began in 1789 when the middle class and working class of France rose against the king and nobility.

During the reign of King Louis XVI (reigned 1774-1793), the nobility of France tried to undermine the king's power and win or keep privileges for themselves. The turmoil and discontent in France grew more and more serious. The upper clergy of the Roman Catholic Church were members of the nobility and often sided with them. The middle class was angry because it was not allowed to take part in government. And workers and peasants were forced to carry an unfair share of taxes and increased living costs.

Some dedicated officials tried to reform the government, but the aristocrats (or nobility) and some wealthy merchants opposed them. In 1789, the government was bankrupt, and the French aristocrats demanded that King Louis XVI call a meeting of representatives from the various classes or "estates" of people. This meeting was called the Estates General and included bishops, aristocrats, and the middle class. Each class had only one vote, but the workers were not represented at all.

The people of the middle class (called the Third Estate) realized that the bishops and aristocrats had no intention of sharing political power with them. So a large number of lawyers representing the Third Estate took over the control of the Estates General when it opened at Versailles on May 5, 1789. They were supported by many parish priests. The Third Estate vowed that they would stay at Versailles and meet until they had provided France with a constitution—a statement of principles that determines the power and duties of the government and the rights of the people. As the weeks passed, the Estates General meeting turned into a National Assembly.

The common workers of Paris came to the aid of the Third Estate. Mobs formed, and on July 14, 1789, they attacked an old fortress named the Bastille. The revolutionary mob saw the Bastille as a symbol of the dictatorial ruling class, because it had been a prison at one time. Also, the revolutionaries also hoped to find weapons in the old fortress. The fall of the Bastille became a symbol of France's struggle for freedom.

The National Assembly, backed by the people, passed many reforms and took away the special rights and privileges of the aristocrats. In August, the Assembly issued the famous "Declaration of the Rights of Man," which declared that all were born and remained free and equal. France had become a constitutional monarchy.

30.

The new government
of France was not hostile
to the Church at first.
But after a few months
of power, the government
moved to take over
Church property in order
to raise money for the
state. Bishops and priests
were now to be employees
of the government and
had to take an oath
of loyalty. Extremists
became very powerful, and
churches and clergy were
often attacked by mobs.

At the start the French Revolution was not hostile to the Roman Catholic religion as such. In fact, many priests supported the revolutionaries' efforts to establish a new social order. One of the first serious breaks came in November 1789. Increasing debts and a growing economic crisis faced the new government. The National Assembly voted to impose an income tax on everyone. It also decided to confiscate church property and to use that wealth to back up its new paper money. Monasteries were shut down, dioceses abolished, and new dioceses created. Bishops and priests were now to be civil employees paid by the government. Clergymen had to swear an oath of loyalty to these measures, which were embodied in the Civil Constitution of the Clergy. The pope, who had not been consulted about these new laws, condemned the civil constitution. It now became very difficult, if not impossible, for a Roman Catholic to support what the French Revolution was doing.

The majority of bishops refused to take the oath, and so did more than half of the lower clergy. Priests who refused to take the oath were outlawed.

Many people felt anger and hatred of the old privileged Church and its aristocratic clergy whose worldly ways had been criticized by Enlightenment thinkers. In the tense atmosphere, suspicions and other emotions exploded into violence against churches, monasteries, and people who had dedicated their lives to the Church. A new sort of intolerance broke out, one which was hardly in line with the thinking of the Enlightenment *philosophes* (thinkers and writers of the French Enlightenment). Extremists were gaining the upper hand. Priests were deported, unless they were hidden by loyal congregations. Monasteries and churches were sacked and destroyed. Many religious men and women were attacked by unruly mobs.

On October 1, 1791, the newly elected Legislative Assembly took control of the French government in accordance with the new constitution of France. The Legislative Assembly was much more radical than the earlier National Assembly had been. The clergy and nobility no longer represented separate Estates, and only very liberal members of these two groups were able to win election to the new government. The following year the king and his family were imprisoned by order of the Legislative Assembly.

31. During a time called
"The Terror" in the French
Revolution, thousands
of people were killed.
Among the victims were
many members of religious
orders. One group was
the nuns of Compiègne,
who were executed because
they would not give up
their religious way of life.

One of the aims of the new extremist French government was to get rid of the Christian religion in France. The government tried to establish a religion dedicated to the Supreme Being, and ordered people to celebrate feasts in honor of Reason and the cycle of nature. The celebrations were sometimes held in churches or cathedrals. Also, people's names and street names were changed, if they were named after saints. Even the names of the months were changed—though they were not religious names to begin with.

In April, 1793, the government established a Committee of Public Safety to safeguard the country's security. Under this committee's rule, France endured a terrible time called The Terror, when thousands of people were condemned to death.

During The Terror, all people of religious convictions were in danger. Religious orders were forced to leave their institutions, and schools and hospitals had to close. Priests were forbidden under pain of death to offer Mass, bishops were put on trial, and lay people could not safely admit that they were Catholic.

Many stories are told of the heroic people who met their death during this time. One group that is especially remembered are the nuns of Compiègne. When their monastery north of Paris was closed down, these nuns continued to meet in small groups in the homes of loyal Roman Catholics. One day they were discovered at prayer, arrested, and thrown into prison in Paris. Though treated with great cruelty, they encouraged the other prisoners and continued their own prayer life. The nuns were brought to trial, and the verdict was known from the start. Chanting the hymn *Veni Creator Spiritus* (Come, Holy Spirit), they were led off to execution.

32. In 1795, France was at war with Austria and Prussia, and the reign of terror had ended. Catholics now felt free to show their faith openly.

Many problems faced the French revolutionary government, including the possibility that other European countries would unite and make war on France. French revolutionaries knew that other monarchies could not let a revolution that deposed its rulers succeed. Besides wanting to fight off any possible enemies, some French leaders wanted to spread their revolutionary ideals of equality and liberty to countries still living under the Old Regime. In November 1792, the National Convention started war against Austria and Prussia.

The war went badly at first but it aroused people's patriotic feelings and thus helped unify the country under the revolutionary government. King Louis XVI, who was a prisoner of the government, was suspected of contacting the enemy. He was tried, condemned, and executed in January 1793.

Under the leadership of Robespierre, Saint-Just, Danton, and Marat, the Committee of Public Safety took control of France in summer 1793. The committee was originally intended to watch over France's security within its own borders. Now it began a reign of terror. Between November 1793 and July 1794, the committee was responsible for the deaths of 13,000 people. Queen Marie Antoinette and more than 1,000 aristocrats were among this group, and about 7,000 were poor people and peasants.

The leaders of the Committee began to struggle for power among themselves. Marat was killed by a citizen, and Robespierre had Danton executed. Soon after that Robespierre himself was tried and executed.

After Robespierre's death in July 1794, things changed for the better. A new constitution was proclaimed in August 1795, and a government called the Directory was established. Ruling power was held by five directors and a legislature. People who paid taxes or served in the army were allowed to vote, but to hold a high office a man had to own land.

Though the laws against religion did not immediately change, people began to be openly religious again. Priests came from their hiding places; other priests returned to France, disguised as travelers or workers. Mass was again offered, and the Roman Catholic Church began to hope that it would again have a secure place in the French nation.

33. Napoleon Bonaparte, a
French general, won many
victories and became
a leading power in the
French government.
He established an
agreement with the pope
called a Concordat.
In 1804, Napoleon became
emperor of France. Pope
Pius VII was present
at the coronation and
expected to crown the new
emperor, but Napoleon put
the crown on his own head.

The closing years of the eighteenth century marked the rise to power of Napoleon Bonaparte. By 1796, he had been given command of the French armies in Italy, where he won a series of great victories. He then determined to weaken England by taking control of the seas leading to India. His armies were victorious in Egypt and Palestine, but Admiral Nelson and his British navy defeated the French fleet in the Battle of the Nile. Napoleon left his army before it was forced to surrender and headed back to Paris in 1799. He was then thirty years old.

In Paris, Napoleon soon got involved in politics. He helped to put down a supposed plot against the government and became one of three consuls appointed to draw up still another constitution. He soon was First Consul under the new government known as the

Consulate. The republican forms of government remained, at least in theory, but Napoleon was the one who really held political power.

Napoleon realized that to gain support he should make peace with the Roman Catholic Church. Pope Pius VII and the French government signed a Concordat in 1801. In it, Catholicism was called the religion of most French people. Parish priests were to be appointed by bishops, but the latter were to be nominated by the First Consul and then ordained by the pope. The Roman Catholic Church was to give up all claims to land that had been taken away from it during the Revolution. Catholic and Protestant clergymen were to be paid by the State, and religious freedom was to be maintained. But the Church was not allowed to be in charge of education again, and priests were not given back the du-

ty of keeping official records of births, deaths, and marriages. France was now the most secularized Roman Catholic country in Europe.

In 1802 Napoleon was named First Consul for life. In 1804 he had himself made a hereditary emperor, a move that was approved by the voters. The pope attended the coronation ceremony, expecting to crown the emperor. But Napoleon seized the crown and put it on his own head and then crowned Josephine, his wife, as empress.

In 1804 Napoleon issued the famous legal code known as the Napoleonic or Civil Code. It was a revised form of the civil laws of France. The *Code Napoléon* has had great influence on law in the Canadian province of Quebec, the American state of Louisiana, Latin America, and almost all of Europe except England.

34. In a set of new laws, Napoleon took control of the Roman Catholic Church in France. He tried to dominate Europe, but in 1814 he was defeated by an alliance of nations.

While still First Consul, Napoleon issued decrees to regulate the Church in France. These decrees (called the Organic Articles) took away many of the gains which the Concordat had seemed to offer the Church. For example, new seminaries could not be built unless the First Consul approved of them. He also had the power to approve regulations in seminaries. Church documents from Rome or a General Council could not be published in France unless the government gave permission. Napoleon forced seminary teachers to

take an oath that included accepting a statement that the General Councils were superior to the pope.

Napoleon's Organic Articles also said that there was to be one catechism and one liturgy for France. There would be no feast days except Sunday. Priests and ministers were no longer allowed to be the state's official witness to a marriage. Couples had to enter into the marriage contract in the presence of a government official before being married in a religious ceremony.

Many lay people, priests, bishops, and the pope himself resisted Napoleon. In 1809, the conflict between the Pope Pius VII and Napoleon became so serious that Napoleon had the pope arrested and taken from Rome. For the next four and one-half years, the pope was in Napoleon's power. But in 1814, Napoleon was defeated by the combined forces of Britain, Prussia, Russia, Spain, and Austria; the pope returned to Rome in triumph.

35. In 1815, representatives of the nations who had defeated Napoleon met at Vienna to arrange a new balance of power in Europe. Many rulers looked favorably on the Church because it could help bring greater stability to their countries. However, the closer ties between Church and government sometimes damaged the Church.

At the Congress of Vienna in 1815 representatives of the powers which had fought and finally defeated Napoleon met to decide the makeup of the new Europe. The ancient republic of Venice came to an end and was put under Hapsburg rule. Germany was made a confederation of thirty-nine states with a diet (a kind of parliament) presided over by Austria. The old Dutch republic was joined with the Austrian Netherlands to form a kingdom under the Prince of Orange. Louis XVIII became ruler of France, which was now surrounded by stronger states. Poland remained divided up among Prussia, Austria, and Russia.

The victorious powers made it clear that they wanted to return to the old order that had prevailed before the French Revolution, but it was not really possible to restore things exactly as they had been. There was now a strong reaction against revolutionary thinking and practice by politicians, rulers, churchmen, and others. The rulers of Austria, Prussia, and Russia signed a treaty binding themselves in a "Holy Alliance." They agreed to conduct the affairs of their countries according to Christian principles. Other kings also joined, but the Holy Alliance had little practical effect and was soon replaced by purely political concerns. But most governments now saw the Roman Catholic Church as an ally of order and stability. An alliance between throne and altar (government and Church) developed in many countries, and papal diplomacy encouraged such ties. With the help of skillful papal diplomats, the Church was successful in improving its position.

France, of course, had been the main scene of the European revolutionary movement. Many people, particularly in the cities, had left the Roman Catholic Church. Now the Church was able to reorganize its life and its religious orders. It could resume its work of education, its parish missions, and other works. The new regime encouraged the tendency toward a national church in France, while the Napoleonic Concordat had actually improved the central power of the papacy.

36. When Pope Pius VII
was free of Napoleon's
power in 1814, he restored
the Society of Jesus.
Now the disbanded Jesuits
were free to return
to their schools and
other institutions and
again take up their work.

The suppression of the Jesuits in the latter part of the eighteenth century had been a serious act. Some thought that among the thousands of exiled and disbanded Jesuits there would surely be acts of rebellion against the Church. Nothing of the sort took place, but Catholic missions and educational work suffered a great deal.

Many of the Jesuits kept hoping that their Society would be restored, and so they kept the spirit of it alive. In Russia, surprisingly enough, Catherine II wanted to keep the two hundred Jesuits who ran the schools in Polish provinces. Pope Pius VI gave his silent consent. During the Reign of Terror in France, a former Jesuit named Peter de la Cloririere had the idea of forming a community which would not wear a distinctive habit or have special structures of its own. (This idea became a reality about 150 years later when the Church approved Secular [or Lay] Institutes.) In Italy Joseph Pignatelli tried to restore a novitiate in the duchy of Parma, but the Napoleonic period had made it impossible.

Better times lay just ahead. One of the first acts of Pope Pius VII when he was released from captivity in 1814 was to officially restore the Society of Jesus. The Jesuits were reunited, but now there were only 600 of them. Many were old, and they bore the scars of their long ordeal. Still, they set to work with energy and enthusiasm. By 1830 there were 2,137 Jesuits, and by 1900 there were 15,073. Their number reached 36,000 in the 1960s.

The role played by the Jesuits in the nineteenth century was very important. Even though they still had to restore their numbers, they played a major role in the Church. Those who wished to attack or undermine the Roman Catholic Church often took aim at the Jesuits as a prime target. But attacks from outside the Church were easier to bear than lack of understanding and support from the Church itself had been.

37.
In the United States, schools were needed to educate the children of Catholic immigrants. The Church there owes much to Mother Elizabeth Seton, who began a religious order of nuns and founded schools for Catholics.

The Catholic Church in the United States faced a serious problem in education in the nation's early years. The majority of Catholics were immigrants, and their children needed to be educated. But public schools at that time in the United States were controlled by Protestants. Here and there in the United States,

schools had been started by religious orders, such as the Ursuline Sisters, the Holy Cross Brothers, and the Christian Brothers. But it was Elizabeth Seton who was mainly responsible for the establishment of Catholic schools on a wide scale and for the common people.

Elizabeth Seton was the wife of William Seton and the mother of five children. She and her husband were devout and active Episcopalians.

In 1803, William Seton died while traveling in Italy with his wife and one of their children. At this sad time, Elizabeth was glad to have the friendship of the Filicchis, an American family living in Italy. She stayed with them for several months and went to Mass with them. At Mass one day she was shocked at the joking remark of an American tourist. She dropped to her knees and began to pray.

Later, at her home in New York, Elizabeth thought about the Catholic churches she had visited in Italy. She studied Catholicism and in 1805 she became a Roman Catholic, to the dismay of her parents and many of her friends. They thought that she was disgracing herself by becoming a Catholic.

Because of their disapproval, Elizabeth moved to Baltimore in 1808. There she opened a school for girls. A year later, with the help of Bishop Carroll and some women, she began a religious order. (Today this order is called the Daughters of Charity.) That same year, Mother Seton (as Elizabeth was now called) and the Sisters moved to Emmitsburg, Maryland, to begin a boarding school for girls. Mother Seton's children were with her, and they helped get the school ready. With the money the Sisters earned from the boarding school they began a free school for poor children in Emmitsburg.

Mother Seton was a strong woman and a good organizer. By the time of her death in 1821, her order had grown tremendously and hundreds of her sisters worked in schools and hospitals. Mother Seton was canonized in 1975; she is the first American-born saint.

Some other religious orders of teaching nuns also began in the United States during the 1800s, including the Sisters of Loreto and the Sisters of Nazareth. Also, thousands of nuns came from Europe to teach in Catholic schools in the United States.

RIO MAGDALENA

CARACAS

RIO ORINOCO

QUITO

LIMA

38. In Latin America, many of Spain's colonies won their independence in the early 1800s. This brought problems to the Roman Catholic Church there because the ruler of Spain had controlled the Church in Latin America. Pope Gregory XVI in 1831 began to correct this problem by appointing bishops for the new nations.

The Spanish colonies in Latin America (South and Central America) had begun to fight for their independence by the end of the eighteenth century. By 1825, many former colonies were now independent nations. Some of these new countries were Bolivia (1825), Chile (1818), Argentina (1816), and Nicaragua (1821).

The new situation in Latin America created various problems for the Roman Catholic Church, some of them stemming from the past. In general, the new governments were basically favorable to the Church. But for centuries the Spanish rulers had enjoyed the right to appoint all the bishops in the colonial dioceses in the New World. There were at least forty Latin American dioceses, and most of the bishops had family ties to Spain. During the wars of independence from Spain, these bishops did not support the rebels, though many parish priests did.

The Roman Catholic Church found itself caught in a difficult position. In Europe, the Church supported legitimate governments. How should it act toward the new governments in Latin America, which had revolted against the mother country? There were other troublesome questions, too. Some of the bishops still felt loyal to Spain. Some of the

new governments wanted to appoint the bishops in their nations, as Spain had done for so long. Some of the priests, especially those who had supported the wars of independence, wanted the Church in Latin America to be in direct contact with the pope in Rome. They wanted the pope to appoint the bishops.

The pope did not move quickly to settle the problem, and things grew worse. Ordinations in Latin America stopped, seminaries were closed, and many dioceses became disorganized. A papal legate (representative) was sent to Latin America to find a way of settling the problems, but the mission was a failure. It was not easy for churchmen in Rome to understand the problems of the Church in such a different, faraway land. Officials in Rome usually looked at things in the light of their experiences in Europe.

When Gregory XVI became pope in 1831, he tackled the problem. He appointed six bishops for dioceses in the new countries of South America. He stated that the Church was concerned for the welfare of souls, so it had the right to deal with governments which were actually in power. Nevertheless, church-state relations remained under severe tension for a long time in many Latin American countries.

39. Romanticism was added to the Enlightenment around 1800, and was especially strong in Germany.

An important new trend called Romanticism was added to that of the Enlightenment at the end of the 1700s. Romanticism, a combination of many ideas and feelings, emphasized emotions and imagination over reason. Here are a few typical Romantic beliefs: Romanticists believed that the world and human beings are infinitely more vast and complicated than had been thought. Everything is constantly growing and changing, they held, and we and every part of nature are constantly becoming different from what we have been. With our imaginations, Romanti-

cists believed, we can create a new world. We have great possibilities for good, but we also have a darker, more evil side. Some Romanticists were attracted to the realm of mystery: the supernatural, melancholy, even the morbid.

Social, political, and religious freedom was important to Romanticists. They were interested in history and in learning about the cultures of foreign nations. Understanding the past and other ways of life might help people form a better future, they thought.

Romanticism was especially strong in Germany, where it found expression in the works of poets, including Johann Wolfgang von Goethe and Friedrich Schiller. It was also prominent in the work of the great German philosopher Georg William F. Hegel (1770-1831), especially in one of his early works, *Phenomenology of Spirit* (1806), in which he presents a philosophical, secular version of the Christian view of history.

In somewhat difficult poetic language, Hegel described Spirit moving out of itself, splintering into opposites, reshaping itself again on higher levels, and eventually returning to itself with all spirits to a state of Absolute Knowing. But until that goal was reached, change and becoming would continue. He said that ideas or systems of ideas develop as one position (thesis) clashes with its opposite (antithesis); out of this clash comes a fusion or harmonization of ideas (synthesis). Hegel's ideas influenced the Marxist, Communist view that workers inevitably clash with rulers and will eventually win out.

Together the Enlightenment and Romanticism may have done more to shape the outlook of Westerners in the nineteenth and twentieth centuries than anything else did.

40. Renewed interest in religion, history, and social work was one of the outgrowths of Romanticism, as is shown by the work of Hofbauer and Schlegel in Vienna.

Romanticism brought to some people a new interest in the sense of mystery, in medieval Christendom, and in the Roman Catholic Church. Some small groups of Romantics explored these matters, and some of them joined the Catholic Church. One lively circle formed in Vienna around 1810, where Clement Mary Hofbauer (1751-1820) and Friedrich Schlegel (1772-1829) worked and taught.

Hofbauer was of a humble Czech family. He needed financial help from others in order to be able to go to the university and study theology. After receiving his degree, Hofbauer went to Rome and joined the Redemptorists, becoming a priest in 1785.

Hofbauer returned to Austria, planning to establish the Redemptorists there. He was stopped from doing this by the laws of the

time against establishing religious houses. So he went to Poland and spent about twenty years there, working among German-speaking people. He devoted himself to helping them grow spiritually and to educational and charitable works.

In 1808, Hofbauer returned to Vienna. There he carried on his mission mainly through hearing confessions and preaching. He was not a great orator, but people flocked to him because he preached very meaningfully about the message of Jesus and the life of grace. Hofbauer was canonized a saint by the Roman Catholic Church in 1909.

Friedrich Schlegel also arrived in Vienna in 1808. Originally from Cologne, Schlegel and his wife had been impressed by the long tradition of the Catholic Church and the cultural heritage of the Middle Ages. They became Roman Catholics the year they moved to Vienna.

Schlegel taught the history of religion in the university at Vienna. In his lectures and his writings he emphasized that European culture owed much to Catholicism and the Roman Catholic Church. He hoped to restore the national life of Austria and Germany according to Roman Catholic traditions.

Schlegel became friendly with Hofbauer and learned about his work for the sick and the poor. Schlegel too became interested in the situation of the poorer classes. He began to call for fairer wages in agriculture and industry. He also began to insist that when economics improved, all should share in the benefits, not merely a few.

41. Liberalism was another important movement in the 1800s. It emphasized progress and freedom, especially in economic and political matters. Liberals opposed alliances between Church and government, fearing that this would encourage the continuance of special privileges for some people.

Liberalism was another important wave of thought which began to take shape in the 1700s and had a strong influence in the 1800s. Liberalism, as the word suggests, emphasizes progress and freedom. It can be applied in many ways. For example, one may hear of a liberal Catholic, or a liberal Protestant.

One of the liberalism's main concerns was with political and economic life. Liberals despised the inefficiency and corruption of Europe's old regimes. They opposed privileges given to the upper classes, and they did not like authoritarian government. Liberals wanted a constitutional government in which the interests of the middle class would be well represented. They wanted all people to be

equal before the law. And they wanted as much freedom as possible in thinking, speaking, forming groups, and making contracts. But the majority of liberals were not in favor of granting everyone the right to vote. Many liberals felt that the middle class should have the largest share of political power. This would, they thought, maintain a balance between the selfish upper classes and the masses of ignorant people at the bottom of the social classes.

Liberals felt that economic freedom was the most important factor in increasing the wealth of the country. Earlier restrictions and regulations should be abolished, and government should interfere with economic freedom as lit-

tle as possible. As time went on, some liberals began to imply that government should have nothing to do at all with social and economic problems.

Liberals also opposed any alliance between Church and the government if that meant continuing old-fashioned ideas and special privileges for some people.

42.
Some Roman Catholics
with liberal ideas tried
to promote the new thinking
within the Church. They
advocated freedom
of the press and schools,
and they wanted the papacy
to stop depending
on the help of rulers.
Some Catholics, such as
Lamennais of France,
left the Church because
their liberals ideas
were condemned.

In the early decades of the nineteenth century, many Roman Catholics wanted to reconcile Christianity and their Church with some of the basic ideas of liberalism. They favored

freedom of speech, freedom of the press, and freedom of worship. Some felt these liberal practices were necessary if the Church was to meet the new needs and demands of the time. Some disliked the close ties between their Church and authoritarian governments. Some people thought that freedom of worship would help their church in Protestant countries, where Roman Catholics were in the minority. And some Catholic thinkers and theologians felt that interest in freedom was rooted in the Christian message.

One of the best-known people who tried to unite the spirit of liberalism with Christian principles was Félicité de Lamennais (1782-1854). A priest and a gifted writer, he wanted both the country's educational system and the Church to be free of the government. A number of enthusiastic, brilliant religious thinkers gathered around him and helped him with his newspaper L'Avenir (The Future) which he published in 1830 and 1831. Lamennais and his co-workers won much support from younger French priests, seminarians, and some laymen. They wanted the papacy to stop depending on temporal power and on the rulers of the nations joined in the Holy Alliance. Instead, Lamennais called for all freedom-loving men to unite. He expected Pope Gregory XVI to lead this fight for freedom. However, the pope condemned Lamennais' ideas.

Lammenais answered with a small book called Words of a Believer. In it, he stated that he believed that the Church had authority in matters of belief, but not in politics. This work, too, was condemned. Lammenais left the Church, but his book was widely read in Europe.

Liberal Catholicism continued in France during the 1830s and 1840s, and in Holland liberal views were expressed in a publication called De Katholiek (The Catholic).

Liberalism was also an important influence in Belgium, which became an independent country in 1831. There the Catholics united with the Liberals and established a constitution that provided freedom of worship, recognition of religious orders, and the appointment of bishops by the pope. However, Church and government were completely separate.

Leopold I (reigned 1831-1865), the king of Belgium, was a Protestant, and his government officials included both Catholics and Protestants. During the next fifteen years, many schools were built in Belgium and liberal laws were passed.

43. The Belgian bishops established a Roman Catholic university in Louvain which became a center of study and knowledge for European nations. Scholars from all over Europe came to lecture at Louvain. At this new university, Roman Catholics could study their Christian and Catholic past and examine new ideas.

The Roman Catholic bishops of Belgium did not trust the moral and religious atmosphere of the state university. So in 1834 they decided to establish a specifically Roman Catholic university in Louvain, which had been a university site for many centuries.

The Belgian bishops did not want to upset Belgian liberals too much, however. Since the latter thought highly of national independence, the bishops decided not to create a pontifical university—that is, a university directly and explicitly dependent on the Church government in Rome. That decision raised fears in conservative Rome, however. The pope worried that the new university in Louvain would become a stronghold of liberal Catholicism. After all, the rector and some other professors shared many of the views of Lamennais, who had publicly turned away from Christianity.

The pope's fears proved groundless. Louvain became a major center of Catholic study and scholarship. Many well-known foreign scholars came to teach at the Roman Catholic university, and they were paid as well as professors in the state university were. Students could be sure that they were getting courses and teachers just as good as those in the state university. Indeed, the first Belgian department of ophthalmology (study of eye diseases) was opened in Louvain's school of medicine.

Cultural studies and oriental languages soon became famous subjects at the university. Its theology professors were also distinguished for their knowledge of the Church Fathers and the thinking of Thomas Aquinas. They used this knowledge to debate other members of the Church who opposed the idea of studying new trends in human life and thought.

The newly organized university arose from a desire among Catholics to study their Christian and Catholic past without being exposed to anti-clerical and anti-Catholic attacks. But defense of the past was not the only reason involved. There was also a desire to face up to new ideas, to see whether and how they might be related to Christian ideas, or how they might even add something new and valuable to Roman Catholicism. Here the example of Thomas Aquinas was very important. He had organized Christian principles, but he had also found much that was valuable for human beings in the thinking of pagan Greek philosophers and others.

In the same way, Roman Catholics who examined the new ideas about political liberty might find ways in which these ideas strengthened the human dignity which Christianity had always taught.

44. At the University of Tübingen, there were both Protestant and Roman Catholic theology departments. John Adam Moehler was a famous Catholic theologian there. He helped people understand that the Church, filled with the life of Christ, was constantly growing. Friedrich Schleiermacher, an important Protestant theologian, also taught at Tübingen. Schleiermacher emphasized the central importance of religion in the life of each person.

At the University of Tübingen in Germany, theology was a lively subject. The university had both a Protestant and a Catholic department of theology, and each had fine teachers.

One such theologian on the Catholic faculty was John Adam Moehler (1796-1838). As a boy, Moehler worked in a bakery and longed to be

able to go to school some day. When his chance came, he was a good student. From his close study of the Church Fathers, Moehler came to see the Church as a living organism. The life of Christ circulated through the Church, and so the Church was constantly growing. Catholic doctrine was not something fixed hard and fast, Moehler believed. Doctrine was meant to help people follow in the footsteps of Christ and to explore the mystery of salvation. Thus Catholic doctrine and dogma were not to be separated from the lives of the faithful; they were meant to be guides and helpmates. Christianity was the revelation that sums up and completes all partial revelations, and church tradition was really the Word of God living in the faithful.

One of the most famous Protestant theologians of the nineteenth century, Friedrich Schleiermacher (1763-1834), was also teaching theology at Tübingen. He seemed to reflect all the currents of thought and feeling that were circulating in the early nineteenth century. He stressed the importance of religion in the intellectual and cultural life of humanity, and he worked out a whole new system of dogmatic theology. The starting point of religion, he said, was the inner feeling of absolute dependence which led human beings towards God as their source.

Protestant and Catholic theologians such as Schleiermacher and Moehler tried to relate their faith to the needs and realities of their time. However, they were not greatly supported by more conservative members of their faiths, who feared that the new ideas would undermine the fixed ideas of their churches. But Catholics and Protestants alike were to find that views like those of Moehler and, to a lesser extent, of Schleiermacher were mild indeed compare to ideas that would develop later in the nineteenth century.

45. In Ireland, Catholics and some Protestants united to resist British rule. Daniel O'Connell, a famous Irish leader, worked tirelessly to restore the political rights of Irish Catholics. In 1829, the Catholic Emancipation Act was passed by the British parliament.

After an Irish attempt at rebellion in 1798, Ireland was forced into a union with Great Britain in 1800. The northeastern province of Ulster had been settled by many Scottish and English Protestants. They enjoyed a privileged position in matters of politics, religion, and economic status both in Ulster, where they were the majority, and in the rest of Ireland, where they were a small minority. Irish Catholics had been deprived of the right to participate in the local parliament, stripped of their landholdings, and forced to pay tithes to support the Protestant Church of Ireland. These were some of the factors which had led to the 1798 revolt by the United Irishmen, whose leaders also included Protestant Irishmen opposed to what was going on in Ireland under British domination. The revolt was severely crushed, and the local Irish parliament was replaced by a United Parliament at London in 1800.

The vast majority of the native Irish were Roman Catholic, and the Catholic Church was a lively force in the country. Maynooth Seminary had been opened in 1795. Native religious congregations such as the Christian Brothers were active. And strong ties existed between the local clergy and the common people. Parish life and the Catholic faith were central in the whole life of the people.

In the year of the revolt, 1798, a young man named Daniel O'Connell became a practicing lawyer in Ireland. He soon got involved in the struggle for the restoration of political rights to Irish Roman Catholics. In 1823 he organized the Catholic Association to work for this goal. It became a powerful force in Ireland, a mass movement which was supported by volunteer workers, villagers, priests, seminarians, and bishops such as Doyle of Kildare.

In 1828 O'Connell was elected to the parliament in London, thanks to the repeal of a British law which forbade the election of Catholics. Another law, however, did not allow him to take the seat in parliament to which he had been elected. Alarmed by growing tension and popular unrest in Ireland, the British government passed the Catholic Emancipation Bill in 1829. Most, but not all, political restrictions against Roman Catholics in Great Britain were removed by this bill.

O'Connell worked tirelessly to change the situation in Ireland. In 1841 he became the first Catholic lord mayor of Dublin since the reign of James II (1685-1688). He kept organizing new grass-roots organizations when the British government outlawed the ones in existence. O'Connell was very much the creator and leader of massive national feeling in Ireland, and he tried to solve Ireland's problems with England by legal means. But as time went on, other Irishmen moved toward more revolutionary solutions.

46. Around 1830 the Oxford
Movement began in the
Church of England.
People in the movement
wanted their church
to be free of parliament.
Also, they wanted
to renew the spiritual
life of their church.
John Henry Newman, one
of the leaders, left
the Church of England and
became a Roman Catholic.

Around 1830, a movement began in the Church of England (the Anglican Church) aimed at bringing back some of the older ideals of faith. The movement centered at Oxford University, and thus it was called the Oxford Movement. Most of the people involved were Church of England priests who wanted to free their church from government control and to renew its spiritual life. Though opposed by Parliament and the press, the movement influenced worship by bringing more ceremony into the Church of England. Also, the Oxford Movement involved the Church of England in helping people who lived in slums. As an outgrowth of the movement, religious orders for the Church of England were revived and religious community life instituted again.

John Henry Newman (1801-1890), an Anglican clergyman, was one of the founders and leaders of the movement. One of the greatest English prose writers, Newman wrote many pamphlets for a series published by the Oxford Movement called *Tracts for the Times*. The tracts described the movement's aims. Newman was famous as a preacher, and a book of his sermons (1834-1842) entitled *Parochial and Plain Sermons* was widely read.

Study of the Church Fathers led Newman to the decision to leave the Church of England and become a Roman Catholic. He was ordained a Roman Catholic priest in 1845 and placed his great literary and intellectual talent at the service of Roman Catholicism. In 1864, Newman wrote an autobiography describing his intellectual development and his conversion to Catholicism. He gave it a Latin title: *Apologia Pro Vita Sua (Explanation of My Life)*. This book is considered a classic of English writing.

47.
In the United States
in the early 1800s,
Roman Catholic immigrants
faced discrimination and
violence, inflamed by a
movement called Nativism.
Religious emphasis in
public schools also caused
conflict. Eventually
these problems were solved.

The Roman Catholic Church in North American grew rapidly in the 1800s. In 1815 there were only 150,000 Catholics in the United States. In 1840 there were 663,000. Twenty years later there were more than 3,000,000.

Catholic immigrants were important in this growth. More than a million and a half Irish came to the United States between 1820 and 1870, and more than half a million Germans. These newcomers brought extraordinary life to American Catholicism. They did not expect government support for their church. A courageous American bishop, John England of Charleston, said: "I am convinced that a total

separation of the Church from the government of the State is the most natural and secure condition for the Church wherever there is not, as in papal territory, a totally ecclesiastical government."

The American Catholic Church faced the difficulty of providing enough priests for the growing Catholic population. Also, the priests and bishops had the difficult task of bringing immigrants of many different national backgrounds together in a peaceful, cooperative group. To help solve this double problem, during the early and mid 1800s the Church in the United States established a network of dioceses, seminaries, parishes, and schools.

Some Americans regarded the coming of the Catholic immigrants as an attempt to establish a foreign religion in the United States. Around 1830, a movement called Nativism became strong in the United States. The Nativists wanted to keep the United States for "native-born Americans," but by that they meant themselves, not the Indians.

Nativists spread false rumors about the Church. In Boston, a sermon by a Nativist preacher inflamed his audience so much that they burned an Ursuline convent near the city.

Another problem that led to bitter conflict was the public schools. At that time, public schools used Protestant prayers and readings from the Protestant version of the Bible as part of the lessons. Some subjects, such as history, included anti-Catholic statements. When Bishop Hughes of New York protested against this, the bitter argument that followed led to riots against the Catholics. The bishop had to put armed guards around his churches to protect them, and Catholics were warned to remain in their homes, away from the mobs. In Philadelphia, too, conflict over schools caused mob action against the Catholics. Eventually, though, the Protestant religion was taken out of the public schools.

To combat false rumors about the Catholic Church, American dioceses and organizations began to publish newspapers and magazines. The first such publication was *U.S. Catholic Miscellany*, started in 1822 by Bishop England.

Most of the violent feelings against Roman Catholics ended at the time of the Civil War (1860-1865). The new Americans served bravely in the army, and this seemed to make the nation accept them.

48. Father John Vianney, the Curé (parish priest) of Ars, France, set an example of pastoral care in the early 1800s. His spiritual leadership transformed his village, and thousands of French people came to him for counsel.

In 1818, John Baptist Vianney traveled to Ars, France, to be its Curé or parish priest. On approaching the village, Father Vianney stopped on a small hill overlooking his parish and prayed for his people. He had heard that the people of Ars seemed to have lost their faith, and he promised to do all he could to bring them back to God.

At that time the Roman Catholic Church in rural France faced many problems. Though religion was still part of people's lives, attendance at church was very low. Now that Church and State were separate, people could disregard church duties without fear of legal punishment or social embarrassment. Some places had been without a priest for a long time

because of the Revolution. Some people in those parishes liked handling their own religious worship and opposed the return of priests. Also, many people complained that village priests charged too many or too high fees for their services.

In Ars, Father Vianney lived humbly and poorly, praying and fasting for the sake of his people. He repaired the parish church himself. Gradually he transformed the religious life of the village, inspiring the people to follow the Gospel message. As the Curé of Ars, Father Vianney became widely known as a confessor, and thousands of French people came to him to receive the sacrament of Penance. He had gifts of insight and understanding that enabled him to help many people in the confessional. A school for girls was another important work begun by Father Vianney, and it became a model in France.

In spite of his great spiritual work, the Curé of Ars was not a person of extensive learning, and he was sometimes spoken of scornfully by other priests and by his superiors. But today he is remembered and honored for his holy, self-giving life, and in 1925 John Vianney, the Curé of Ars, was declared a saint by the Roman Catholic Church and the patron of parish priests.

49. Gregory XVI condemned slavery and the slave trade in 1839. This decree was part of his overall effort to encourage missionary activity among black people. In 1841, Franz Libermann began a missionary order to work in Africa.

"It is forbidden to any Catholic, priest or lay person, to maintain that the slave trade and slavery are legitimate." With these words Pope Gregory XVI condemned slavery in his Apostolic Constitution entitled *In supremo* (December 3, 1839).

Slave trade had been going on among Africans before European merchants arrived in the fifteenth and sixteenth centuries. But the Europeans greatly expanded the business, supplying Black slaves to the colonies and plantations of the Americas.

In condemning slavery, Gregory XVI was repeating the church teaching that had been maintained by some earlier popes, priests, and scholars: e.g., Paul III, Pius V, Urban VIII, Benedict XIV, Francisco Suárez, Bartolomé de Las Casas, and Peter Claver. During the eighteenth century many people of good will including French and English thinkers of the Enlightenment, began to challenge the rightness of slavery. Many large nations began to rule against slavery at the close of the eighteenth century and during the nineteenth century progressed: Denmark in 1792, France in 1794, the Congress of Vienna in 1815, and the British Empire in 1833. In 1841 an agreement to suppress the trade in Black Africans was signed by France, England, Russia, Austria, and Prussia. The importation of African slaves was prohibited after 1808 by the United States statute. But cotton-growing in the southern states favored the use of slaves and created an issue that would be resolved only by the Civil War.

Gregory XVI's condemnation of slavery was part of his overall effort to stimulate missionary efforts. In his missionary instruction entitled *Neminem profecto* (1845), he made clear the two solid bases of the Church's preaching of the gospel message: the ongoing establishment of local churches and the training of native clergy. Efforts were made to organize the missions more carefully, to parcel out mission territories among various religious orders, and to establish the proper lines of authority.

An important figure in this new missionary effort was Franz Maria Libermann, a Jewish convert to Roman Catholicism. When he entered the French seminary at Issy, he heard of the plight of Africans from two seminarians. With the support of Bishop Luquet, Libermann and his two friends founded the Missionaries of the Sacred Heart of Mary in 1841 to work among Blacks. In the next two years they were sent as missionaries to the islands of Mauritius and Réunion in the Indian Ocean. In 1843 ten missionaries of this order arrived in Dakar (Senegal), where Mother Javouhey (1779-1885) had sent some of her nuns as early as 1819. But the tropical climate soon defeated the missionaries.

New members continued to join the order, which soon united with another group to form the Holy Ghost Fathers. More than 2,000 of them would spread out over the African continents in the years to follow. Libermann offered this wise advice: "Become Blacks with Blacks. Don't train them as Europeans. Let them keep what is theirs. Go before them as servants before your masters."

50. The government of Korea did not allow Christian missionaries into the country, but the Christian faith was spread by two Christian converts. The Church grew, in spite of persecutions. In 1880 Christianity became legally tolerated in Korea.

One of the countries where Christianity entered only with great difficulty was Korea. During the Japanese occupation of Korea between 1592 and 1599, a few Christian soldiers had baptized some native children. Later a few Korean slaves in Japan became Christian and suffered martyrdom. But until the end of the eighteenth century there was no Korean Church. Foreigners were not allowed into the country, and it was easy to catch and eliminate foreign missionaries.

In 1777 a book about Christianity and the gospel message happened to fall into the hands of a Korean scholar named Piek-i. He

became interested in Christianity. Learning that his friend, Ri-Seung, was going to Peking to pay his annual respects to the Chinese emperor, he asked him to contact Christian missionaries there. Ri-Seung did so and became a Christian convert. When he returned to Korea, he baptized Piek-i. The two began to preach the Christian faith enthusiastically among educated and uneducated Koreans. When the first priest, a Chinese named James Tsiu, came to Korea in 1795, he found about 4,000 Christians there. In 1809 a terrible persecution brought martyrdom to Father Tsiu and about 300 other Christians. But the faith remained alive among the 10,000 or more Christians living in Korea.

In 1834 another Chinese priest arrived, to be followed soon afterwards by a vicar apostolic and two French missionaries. Severe persecution broke out again in 1839 and between 1866 and 1868. Toleration of Christianity came only after 1880. By World War I there were somewhere between 65,000 and 75,000 Roman Catholics in Korea.

Protestant missionary work in Korea began seriously after 1880. It devoted much attention to education, medical care, and public health projects. By 1914 there were about 100,000 Protestants in Korea. Three-fourths were Presbyterians, and about one-fourth were Methodists.

China

Peking

Macao

51. In China, Jesuit missionaries wanted to include ancient Chinese customs in Christian religious ceremonies, but the Roman Catholic Church would not allow it.

Ever since the 1200s, Roman Catholic missionaries of various orders had worked in China. They disagreed among themselves about whether ancient Chinese customs should become part of Christian religious ceremonies. The Jesuits wanted the Chinese to keep their cultural practices after they became Christians, but some other orders objected.

Church government in Rome ruled against the Jesuits, and this made the Chinese angry. The rulers now regarded missionaries and Christians as possible allies of foreign and unfriendly countries. They no longer supported or protected the missionaries, and their work was slowed down greatly.

Still, by the beginning of the 1800s there were about 250,000 Christians in China, several dozen missionaries, and about 50 Chinese priests. Missionaries continued to arrive. In 1835 Jean Perboyre, a French priest, traveled through China in disguise. In his letters, he described the difficult life of Christians in China. After four years' work, he was arrested, tried, and executed, along with some Chinese Christians.

Around the middle of the nineteenth century, Great Britain and France established "treaty ports" with China. In these cities foreigners could live and practice their own religion. These treaties were mainly to increase commerce for the European countries, but they did provide greater opportunity for mission work.

The first Protestant missionary, Robert Morrison, came to China in 1807 and had made ten converts before his death in 1834. By 1850 there were still only about 100 converts to Protestantism. But ahead lay a great era of Protestant missionary work in China.

52.
The work of evangelizing Oceania was begun in 1835 by Pierre Chanel, a French priest.

In 1836 a missionary expedition sailed the southern seas on a course towards Futuna Island, which lies more than 3,000 kilometers (1860 miles) from Australia. The missionaries belonged to the Society of Mary, a new missionary group that had arisen in Lyons, France. The Picpus Fathers had reached Honolulu in 1827, but a vast missionary field still lay untouched in Micronesia and Melanesia. It was to this unknown region that Pope Gregory XVI had sent the Society of Mary.

In the expedition was Pierre Chanel, a thirty-six-year-old priest who had been a parish priest and the superior of a seminary. Accepting the proposal of the expedition leader, Chanel and a companion landed on the island of Futuna with their few belongings. While struggling to adapt to the new climate and culture, Chanel studied the local language, prepared a little dictionary, tended the sick, and preached the gospel message.

Some natives became converts. At first the chief of the local tribe, Niuliki, had welcomed the priest. Now he grew fearful that the priest would take away his authority and undermine

local religious practices. When Niuliki's first-born son asked to be baptized, the chief decided to have the missionary killed. His chief minister, Muzu-Muzu, was given the task. Summoned to help a sick person, Chanel was attacked with clubs by Muzu-Muzu and his henchmen. He died on April 28, 1841.

Six months later a French ship arrived to recover Chanel's remains. To his surprise the captain found that the natives were not openly hostile. Indeed, a group of them approached him and asked him to send another missionary. One year later more than half of the island's population had been baptized. Even Muzu-Muzu was converted, and he asked to be buried near the spot where he had killed Pierre Chanel.

53. Many new religious orders were formed in the 1800s, and some old ones came back to life. In France, Lacordaire reorganized the Dominicans, and Dom Guéranger re-established the abbey of Solesmes to restore the Benedictine way of life in France.

During the Enlightenment period, many people questioned the usefulness of religious orders. Moreover, they looked on monasteries and convents as cozy havens for younger sons and daughters of the nobility, and church offices seemed to be designed for noblemen. By the second half of the eighteenth century, for example, all French bishops and archbishops came from noble families. Religious life was on the decline, and only the poor parish priests kept the affection of their people.

In the nineteenth century, by contrast, new religious orders for men and women flourished as never before. At least eighty-eight communities for men were founded, and women religious set out to tackle the many and varied duties which Vincent de Paul had pictured for them in the seventeenth century. These women were to be found in hospital wards, on battlefields, in educational work, and by the side of lepers and others with incurable diseases.

Older orders also were revitalized. We have read about the restoration of the Jesuits and its good effects for the Roman Catholic Church. Here we shall read about developments in France which were encouraged by Pope Gregory XVI and which proved important for the Church. One was the work of Father Lacordaire for the Dominican Order;

the other was the foundation of the Bendictine Abbey of Solesmes by Dom Guéranger.

Lacordaire had been a friend and associate of Lamennais on the journal *L'Avenir* but he did not follow him out of the Church. Lacordaire had also won great fame as a preacher for the Lenten sermons which he preached in Notre Dame Cathedral in Paris. In 1838 he became a Dominican and announced his plan to restore the Dominican Order in France, where it had been suppressed since 1790. Lacordaire stressed the importance of guiding the education of young people, preaching, and new activities that would meet the needs and ideas of the day. He gathered many followers around him, and by 1850 it was possible to establish a Dominican province in France.

Around the same time in France, Dom Guéranger was busy with his plan. His life and work are a good example of Romanticism in action. He thought a good deal about the great centers of monastic culture that had existed in the Middle Ages, and he and some companions decided to settle in the old priory of Solesmes. Guéranger wished to restore the primitive rule and monastic practices of St. Benedict. Among other things, the Abbey of Solesmes led the way in reviving pure Gregorian chant, which is now regarded as an important part of the West's musical heritage.

54. Immense changes came to Western civilization during the time of the Industrial Revolution.

By the end of the eighteenth century, the Industrial Revolution was well under way in England. The term "Industrial Revolution" refers to all the changes that took place in western civilization when hand tools were replaced with power-driven machines. The Industrial Revolution spread to North America, Belgium, and France over the next fifty years, and even more slowly to other parts of Europe.

Machines were not new to Europe. For centuries hand-powered machines had been used in the shops of craftsmen and in the homes of peasants. There were looms and other machines for making textiles. Machines were also used in mills, mines, and many kinds of work, and the products were sold with the help of traders and merchants. The labor was called "cottage industry" because it was done at home or in one's local surroundings. It was usually part-time work, and farming remained the major work activity.

During the eighteenth century there was greater interest in organizing production for more speed and higher quantity. Scientific work suggested that much could be discovered, improved, and invented. There was a revolution in the application of new energy sources, especially steam. Work that had been done by hand—such as weaving—now was done by machine.

In 1793 Eli Whitney developed a machine called the cotton gin to separate cotton fiber from cotton seeds. This made it possible to get

raw cotton quickly and cheaply, and cheap cotton cloth became a possibility.

Big, heavy machinery meant that the days of cottage industry were on their way out. Workers were collected into large buildings, called factories, that housed the machinery. Interchangeable parts for machines and tools began to be used, and this made it easier to produce goods on a massive scale. With more workers on the job, more goods could be produced and sold, and at a cheaper cost. Before the Industrial Revolution, most goods produced were for the wealthy classes. Now production provided cheap goods—clothing, housing, transport, food—for the working class as well.

Workers for the factories were drawn from the farms to the work sites in cities, where power for the machines was available. Cities grew rapidly. For example, the English towns of Liverpool and Manchester had fewer than 15,000 people each in 1750. One hundred years later, Manchester had more than 300,000 people, and Liverpool almost 400,000.

55. Cities grew quickly as workers left rural areas to work in factories. Living conditions in cities were very bad, but the Industrial Revolution did improve the welfare of workers in some ways.

What about the people who gathered to work in the new industrial cities, such as Liverpool and Manchester in England? What effects did the Industrial Revolution have on their lives? Was the Industrial Revolution a good thing or bad thing for the working people of Europe?

There were many facts on the bad side. Factories were noisy, hot, dirty, unpleasant, poorly aired, and dangerous to health. People had to work six days a week, usually from sunrise to sunset or longer. Many of these workers were women and children. They had little or no say in dealing with their bosses, who were really dictators on the job. There was no great comfort in going home to some dwelling in the city either. Workers and their families were crowded into narrow rooms, and more than a few lived in cellars. One, two, or even three families might live in a single room. The industrial cities themselves were smoky, dirty, and boring. There were none of the play-

grounds or amusements we now picture for children in any big city. Group awareness was only slowly beginning to dawn on workers as they trooped to factories, lounged in meeting halls, met on soup lines, and read leaflets written and printed by fellow-workers, socialists, or clergymen. A young German businessman in England described the situation as he saw it around 1844. He was Friedrich Engels (1820-1895), the long-time friend and co-worker of Karl Marx. His book, *The Condition of the Working Class in England,* has remained a classic description of the situation.

Looking back now, we can say that conditions were terrible in many respects. But were they terrible by comparison with the lives of others on farms and in villages? Was the Industrial Revolution to blame for making things worse for people? The answer to both questions seems to be "no." Men, women, and children on farms worked long hours too, and they often lived on the edge of starvation.

Their cottages were no better than city dwellings. The picture of happy, contented farm life is false, if you start examining the lives of real farm people in western Europe at this time.

The population of Europe began to rise rapidly from the middle of the eighteenth century on. People also lived a bit longer. Some improvements in medical care probably helped, but it now seems clear that better nutrition—better food and eating habits— were the main reason for the increase in population. These improvements in living conditions came as a result of the Industrial Revolution. Also, wages of skilled workers rose in the nineteenth century, so some workers were better off than before.

But what, if anything, would the various Christian Churches do about the problems of the industrial workers, also known as the proletariat?

56.

The Christian Churches as institutions were slow to work on the problems connected with industrial life in the city. But individual Christians tried to help. Frédéric Ozanam, a Frenchman, founded the St. Vincent de Paul Society to help the unemployed and disabled. In England, a group of Anglicans began Christian Socialism.

On the whole the Christian Churches did not officially take serious notice of the plight of industrial workers in the first part of the nineteenth century. Some groups, such as the Methodists and Quakers, however, kept in touch with the lower classes. Roman Catholic priests in the United States also maintained ties with the working classes, from which many of them had come. But early organizations of workers were usually secular in nature, though Christian doctrine might influence the thinking of their leaders and members. For example, the worker reform movement in England known as Chartism

(1838-1848) was aimed at helping workers, and various forms of Socialism were beginning to spread in Europe.

A movement motivated by Christian ideas was begun by Frédéric Ozanam (1813-1853). He was a French Catholic scholar who also played an important part in trying to promote Catholic social theory and action. With the help of friends, and particularly of a nun named Rosalie Rendu, he organized what would become the St. Vincent de Paul Society. At this time society did not provide anything for the unemployed or disabled. Children, the aged, and the sick depended on families or friends, and many were not cared for. The work of Ozanam and his followers among the poor and needy was urgently needed.

Ozanam tried to awaken Catholics to economic and social problems. "It is not God who makes poor people," he wrote. He attacked selfish profiteers who did not allow laborers to benefit fairly from the work they contributed to industry. In the newspaper *L'Ere Nouvelle (The New Era),* he urged Roman Catholics to get involved in social issues and problems. He did not want things left in the hands of government that would serve only the rich and the cause of profit-making.

Christian Socialism was another religion-motivated movement. It began in England in 1848. Protestants, including John Ludlow, Frederick Maurice, and Charles Kingsley, wanted the working classes and the Christian Church to oppose capitalism. They published articles and pamphlets, organized labor associations, and founded a college for workingmen. Maurice was also a founder of Queen's College for women (1848). He and Kingsley, who were Anglican clergymen, also tried to get their ideas across in works of fiction. Kingsley wrote a famous children's book, *The Water Babies* (1863), a fantasy about little Tom, a boy chimney sweep who falls into a river and becomes a new kind of person, a water baby. This book was enjoyed as a story but it also showed the plight of poor children.

Some of the ideas of Christian Socialism had a strong influence on American Protestantism towards the ends of the nineteenth century.

57. In 1848, many nations, provinces, and states of Europe rebelled against their rulers, demanding better living conditions and more participation in government. As a result, more nations came under constitutional governments.

In the 1840s, there were many social, economic, and political problems in Europe. The lower middle and working classes wanted better living conditions and more participation in government. Also, a rising spirit of nationalism swept through some regions. People wanted their countries to be united under one government instead of being split up into states and provinces ruled by princes, or sometimes by a foreign power.

In 1848, the various tensions exploded into uprisings in many parts of Europe. Within the first three months, rulers of four Italian provinces were forced to grant constitutions. In February, the people of Paris drove out King Louis-Philippe and created the Second Republic. In March there were uprisings in Hungary, Prague, Vienna, Heidelberg, and Berlin. The people of Milan and Venice drove out their Austrian rulers.

The Papal Territory in Italy was one of the provinces in which revolution had been simmering a few years earlier. This region ruled by

the pope stretched across central Italy and included the city of Rome. Pope Pius IX, who became pope in 1846, granted a liberal constitution to the people. His problems seemed headed for a peaceful solution, but in 1848 revolutionaries from outside incited violent uprisings in Rome. Pope Pius IX fled to Naples, and a republic was declared in Rome. The disorders continued, and a dictatorship was set up in March 1849. French troops came to the pope's aid, and the Papal Territory was restored to him in 1849. Pius IX returned to Rome, where he ruled the Papal Territory for the next eleven years.

In France, after Louis-Philippe was removed, many workers, socialists, and some Catholics continued to demand social justice. They were convinced that the living conditions of the common people should be improved and that property should be distributed more fairly. The workers' movement became violent and led to a bloody uprising in June 1848. The archbishop of Paris lost his life trying to calm the revolutionaries. Many French Catholics were conservative, and the violence prompted others who had supported the movement for social justice to withdraw their help. Only a few liberal Catholics in France now supported democratic ideals.

As is often the case with revolutions, the uprisings of 1848 were not the work of entire peoples rising against a tyrant. They were the work of well-organized minority groups who had high confidence in their ideals. In France, the revolution succeeded. In other regions, such as Milan, Vienna, and Prague, the Austrian rulers put the revolutions down. And in some places, constitutional governments emerged, which were an improvement over the absolute monarchies and enlightened despotism that had been in power. Another result of the revolutions was that in France and elsewhere in Europe, the Roman Catholic Church lost its hold on members of the working class. Many workers now believed that the Church was allied with the ruling class.

58. In the Slavic areas of Europe, the movement for freedom was very strong. Among the Poles, Adam Mickiewicz, a poet and a man of action, urged his people to renew their spiritual life. This renewal, he and many other Poles hoped, would spread throughout all Europe.

In Slavic areas of Europe the political ideals and movements of the time were felt with great intensity. Because of the settlements reached at the Congress of Vienna in 1815, none of the Slavic peoples except the Russians was free of foreign control. The Serbs and Bosnians in the south, who were Orthodox for the most part, were under Turkish domination. The Croats were in the kingdom of Hungary, which in turn was part of the Austrian empire of the Hapsburgs. The Bohemians, too, were under the Hapsburgs. Poland was divided among three powers: the Hapsburgs, Russia, and Prussia.

The Slavic peoples had preserved their spoken languages, their traditional songs, and their culture. Some of them, such as the Poles of Warsaw, had also managed to preserve some of their laws and political institutions.

As we noted earlier, Romanticism encouraged fresh interest in the cultural past of peoples and nations, and particularly in past moments of greatness and independence. In the early part of the nineteenth century, therefore, efforts were made here and there to collect old folk songs, to study Slavic languages and cultures, to publish texts and documents, and to create scientific or cultural journals. These efforts soon took on broad political and cultural overtones.

It became clear that there were many points of contact and relationship among the various Slavic peoples. They had closely related languages, similar histories, and probably a common origin. Now almost all of them were oppressed. Perhaps they should unite to win liberation together. Many intellectuals and statesmen were drawn to the image of a feder-ation which would include all the Slavic peoples. This current of thought and action was called Pan-Slavism.

The Poles tended to move beyond such notions to a broader vision, and Polish spokesmen combined strong national tradition and religious ideals with their human freedom. It found powerful expression in the great poetry of Adam Mickiewicz (1798-1855), who was also an organizer and man of action. Many Poles hoped that a profound spiritual renewal of mind and heart could start in Poland and spread to other nations. Perhaps it could lead to an era of true peace and brotherhood. This basic attitude probably underlay the work of many Poles who struggled for freedom in their own country and elsewhere throughout the nineteenth century.

59. In the mid-nineteenth century, there was much disagreement about how the Christian Churches should adjust to the changing times. Rosmini, an Italian, discussed the problems of the Roman Catholic Church in a famous book.

The Christian churches, following Jesus' example, try to be in the world and yet not of the world. This is a very difficult thing to accomplish, because, although the Church has a divine mission which is timeless, it also has a human side which places it in the midst of ever-changing times. The adjustment between the Church and the world goes on constantly, and this is a process about which Christians often disagree among themselves.

A few years after the revolutions of 1848 an Italian priest named Antonio Rosmini (1797-1855) had some ideas about how the Church should adjust to the world of the middle of the nineteenth century. He wrote a book called *The Five Wounds of the Church.* In it he said that the Church was hurt by too much dependence on the state and by failing to modernize some of its old-fashioned attitudes toward the place of the laity in the Church. He pointed to the recent revolutions as an example of a new spirit of democracy and freedom in the world, and he said that the Church should adjust itself to this important new spirit. Though many people agreed with Rosmini, many others thought his ideas were shaking people's belief in the divine character of the Church, and they urged the pope to condemn the book. In the end the pope did not condemn it, but he did not approve it either.

It is easier to see now than it was then that much of what Rosmini said made good sense. The freedom of the individual and of institutions is very much in harmony with the truths of Christianity. But many Christians in 1850 felt that the freedom Rosmini praised was a threat to Christian faith. They pointed out such things as the following to support their view. The freedom of scientists led to widespread doubts about the Bible's doctrine of creation. Some theologians, especially in Germany, were using their freedom to describe Jesus as only a myth. The liberal governments in Belgium and parts of Italy would not let the Church share in the education of children. The democracy in the United States permitted persecution of Catholics and Mormons. In many Latin American countries revolutionary leaders seemed to want to get rid of Christianity.

So there was much disagreement about how the Christian Churches should adjust to the changing world, and that disagreement would continue.

Outline by Chapter

The Church in Revolutionary Times

Chapters 2, 17, 39, and 55 written by John Drury.
Chapter 59 written by Marvin R. O'Connell.